SO-BZA-444

Fighting
the Black Beast

Overcoming your depression

MICHAEL L. WALTON

SAFFRON WALDEN
THE C.W. DANIEL COMPANY LIMITED

First published in Great Britain in 1990
by The C.W. Daniel Company Limited
1 Church Path, Saffron Walden
Essex, CB10 1JP, England

© Michael L. Walton 1990

ISBN 0 85207 220 1

Designed by Peter Dolton.

Design and Production in association
with Book Production Consultants, Cambridge, England.

Typeset by Anglia Photoset, Colchester
Printed and bound by St. Edmundsbury Press Ltd., Bury St. Edmunds, Suffolk.

CONTENTS

Acknowledgements

My thanks to the following for copyright material,

"The Bhagavad Gita" Penguin Classics, 1962
Translated by Juan Mascaró, and edited by Betty Radice.
Reproduced by permission of Penguin Books Ltd.

"The Ramayana and The Mahabharata"
Translated by Romesh C. Dutt.
Everyman's Library, J.M. Dent & Sons Ltd.

"Bring Out the Magic in Your Mind" by Al Koran
A. Thomas & Co. (Thorsons Publishing Group Ltd)

"Karmic Laws" by Dr Douglas Baker BA, MRC; LRCP; FZS.
The Aquarian Press (Thorsons Publishing Group Ltd.)

INTRODUCTION

DEPRESSION IS AN ILLNESS, not just a state of mind. It is not something you can pull yourself out of overnight, although people who gaily tell sufferers to "pull themselves together" and "cheer up" seem to think so. Of course you want to cheer up, who wants to be depressed? But you don't know how to go about it.

Just trying to be cheerful in the midst of acute depression is useless. Much, much more needs to be done to drive away the dark clouds that have thrown a shadow over your life.

I have been depressed, and I still suffer from it, for it is a chronic illness you have to learn to live with, much like diabetes and arthritis. I have also known quite a number of other sufferers so it is an illness I am all too familiar with.

Depression is like a black cloud hanging over you, blotting out the sun. It is like being alone in perpetual twilight, with a nameless fear gnawing away inside you. The world appears to echo your mood, all the colours fading to grey. Grey buildings, grey streets, grey skies, grey people. When the sun does shine it appears to be mocking you. Depression is a sort of living death where all vitality and enthusiasm for life has been sucked out of you and you are left empty and drained.

Robert Frost in "The Death of the Hired Man" said:

"And nothing to look backward to with pride,
And nothing to look forward to with hope."

Another view of depression is given by Sara Teasdale in "The Broken Field":

"My soul is a dark ploughed field
In the cold rain;
My soul is a broken field
Ploughed by pain."

In depression there arises within the sufferer a yawning emptiness. The future is a dark unknown that seems to offer nothing other than deepening despair, and the past is a nightmare full of ghosts that come back to haunt you in the early hours of the morning. Death is ever present – a spectre that lurks in the shadows of your world, beckoning to you with a skeletal hand, urging you to give up your struggle and accept defeat. Everything has become pointless and hopeless. There is no pleasure in life, only pain.

Other people's happiness is like an insult to you. You hate Christmas and weddings because you cannot bear to see other people so happy while you are lonely and miserable. You may find yourself thinking, "Damn them! I hope something really horrible happens to them to wipe that superior grin off their smug faces. Then they will know what I'm going through." Bitterness towards anybody who is happy is common in depression and is one of the most destructive aspects of the illness.

Weddings can be avoided, but Christmas is an annual nightmare that must be endured. If you are unemployed or living on the breadline Christmas seems to have the sole purpose of mocking your poverty. Jewellery shops glittering with golden gifts so far beyond your means that the prices are a joke. Electronic goods you could never afford in a million years. You don't celebrate Christmas any more because you do not have anything to celebrate, do you? And all these happy people just make you feel more alienated than ever. Tragically, many people commit suicide around Christmas time.

When life becomes more frightening than death then suicide may be seen as the only answer. There are two forms of suicide; the "token" suicide and the completed suicide. Token suicides are more common in women than men, while in men a suicide attempt is more likely to be successfully completed. The token suicide is a "cry for help" and the person is saying to the world, "Look how unhappy I am. Look how desperate I have become. Now will you take me seriously?" She doesn't really want to die – just ruffle a few feathers and make people take notice of her. She is careful to ensure that she is found, and may even tell people she is going to attempt suicide.

The methods chosen for token suicide are usually overdoses or slashing the wrists. My aunt, a lifelong depressive, phoned me one morning and just said, "I've got some tablets in my hand and I'm going to take them." I got the Samaritans to keep her talking while I rushed over, only to find her smiling and saying, "I feel better now." She had achieved her objective and had all the attention she wanted.

The completed suicide is more usual in men. In this case, the person really wants to die and takes pains to ensure that he will not be interrupted. He locks himself away – or goes to some lonely place – and coolly works out how he is going to execute the suicide and then goes ahead with it. He may or may not leave a suicide note. I knew a farmer who appeared to be quite normal and level-headed, but this was merely a guise to hide a deeply troubled soul. One day he just walked out to his barn and hanged himself.

It is important to recognise the warning signs and know when suicide is being contemplated. Never take threats of suicide lightly. Sit down and talk to the person and offer your support. Show you genuinely care. Hints of suicide may come in some carefully chosen words, such as, "It would be better for everybody if I wasn't here", or "Nobody cares if I live or die", and finally, "I can't go on".

Unfortunately, the all to common response is, "Oh don't be silly." The depressed person is not being silly. They may be deadly serious. Such unconcerned brush-offs may actually make the person more determined than ever to go through with it because he or she believes nobody cares. Never mock a suicidal person, and NEVER make them feel guilty by saying things like, "How can you do this to me?"

What a potential suicide wants more than anything is for somebody to reach out to them with open arms, offering love, friendship, and a sympathetic ear. It is not necessary to say anything other than, "It's alright now, I'm here" and *BE THERE*.

Sooner or later a severely depressed person will be sent to see a psychiatrist. Now while psychiatrists undoubtedly help some of their patients, they cannot wave any magic wands. Stubborn cases may be admitted to hospital and even given ECT treatment. The problem is that once the patient has lost control over his or her own mind, they look to the psychiatrist for a miracle. When that miracle does not happen they lose faith in the medical profession and may get more depressed than ever. Then strong drugs are used and these make the world seem even more unreal and even more nightmarish than it already is. The psychiatrist's big mistake is that he (or she) imagines his methods are infallible and will not admit he is defeated. He prefers to make the patient feel it is his fault!

Psychiatrists do tend to specialise to the detriment of the unfortunate patient. For instance, the patient may first be sent to a psychiatrist of the Freudian school who interprets all his problems as being the result of an overbearing mother or repressed sexuality. Then when this line of treatment fails to produce results, the patient is sent to a psychiatrist of the

7

Jungian school, who dismisses everything the first psychiatrist said and makes a new interpretation of the patient's problems. Next the patient may be sent to an Adlerian psychiatrist and so on. You can guess how confusing all this is to the patient, and in the end, with some justification, he may dismiss all psychiatrists, saying that none of them have a clue.

Patients on psychiatric treatment must realise that psychiatrists can offer a sympathetic ear, and some guidance, but they cannot cure you. In the end you will realise that you must cure yourself. And that is where this book will help you.

Anyone suffering from nerves or depression will be prescribed some form of medication. In the past barbiturates were popular, and then the benzodiazapines such as Valium, Ativan and Librium. These were highly addictive drugs and have caused more problems than they have cured, although people with acute anxiety do need something. Never take benzodiazapine drugs in regular doses every day or you will become addicted to them. Take them as infrequently and as erratically as possible so your body never has the chance to develop a craving for them. Also, reduce your dose to the absolute minimum. I have taken 5 milligrams of Diazapam (Valium) once a day, although I quite often miss a day, for many years and have not become addicted to them. I believe this is only because I ignored the doctor's original instructions to take one three times a day which would have led to addiction.

There are alternatives to tranquillizers. Herbal preparations such as Lanes' "Quiet Life" pills are very good, and contain non-addictive herbs. Passiflora tablets are also an excellent natural remedy. Then there are herbs such as chamomile, scullcap, valerian, lime blossom and hops. Many of these are in the herbal tables, but they can be bought separately as dried herbs or tea bags. A severely anxious person would be well advised to avoid stimulating drinks such as tea and coffee and drink these herbal teas instead.

If you are on drugs of any kind, remember that the drugs themselves may contribute to your symptoms and make you feel worse, not better. There may come the day when, drugged up to the eyeballs, and faced with admittance to hospital and ECT treatment, you call "enough" and decide to take charge of your own life and try to cure your depression yourself. This is the time to begin the following Eight Point Anti-Depression Plan.

The Plan is based on esoteric and alternative principles as well as conventional ones, so some parts of it may seem strange and appear to have nothing to do with depression, but bear with it! Everything that is included in the plan is there for a very good reason.

I believe this is the first time a treatment for depression (and to a lesser degree anxiety) has been devised that uses esoteric principles. I can only say that, like acupuncture, although we do not fully understand how it works, it works! There is nothing to lose and everything to gain, so go into the Plan with an open mind and the determination to succeed and banish depression from your life once and for all.

CHAPTER ONE

KNOW YOUR ENEMY

MILLIONS OF PEOPLE have had their lives wrecked by nervous illness. All too often it is dismissed as a "trivial" problem, when in fact it can be as debilitating as cancer and just as worrying for relatives. In the case of depression it is just as life-threatening due to the ever-present risk of suicide.

Depression is no respector of persons and attacks people of both sexes and in all walks of life. There is evidence that it runs in families, and that there is a gene for it hiding within the forty-six chromosomes that make up a human being. It can therefore be looked upon as a congenital disease – that is, it is present at birth.

While anyone can become temporarily depressed – if they suffer a bereavement for instance – severe long-term pathological depression is something else, and it is present all the time, summer or winter, rain or shine. In chronic depression there is always a dark cloud hanging over you, a shadow on the sun, a nameless fear gnawing away in the pit of your stomach, and a feeling of hopelessness and unreality.

Depression can lie dormant for many years like a sleeping volcano, only manifesting as an unusually "sensitive" disposition, and then some crisis releases the Black Beast and it overwhelms you. The trigger can be a bereavement; a physical attack; a car accident; the loss of a job; hormonal changes in women, or even the birth of a baby.

I knew one middle-aged lady who was perfectly all right until an over-zealous dentist removed all her teeth. The loss of her teeth prevented her eating properly and no dentures ever seemed to fit her without causing pain. She began to drink to numb the pain and gradually she became deeply depressed. Eventually, in spite of medication, psychiatric treatment, and weeks in a mental hospital, she drank herself to death. It might seem illogical that the loss of one's teeth should result in severe depression, but this case is by no means unusual.

The genetically depressive person is balanced on a knife-edge, and it doesn't take very much to push them over onto the slippery slope that leads ever downwards, through deeper and deeper depression, to suicide.

A man I knew, always a good conversationalist, and apparently full of enthusiasm for life and the kind of person described as "a tonic", changed completely after a car accident and became deeply depressed. From being the life and soul of any party, he became a recluse, hiding in his bedroom when visitors called so he would not have to see them.

The event that acts as the trigger does not have to be particularly earth-shattering – it can be something that a less sensitive person would take in their stride. The menopause for instance can cause depression and/or anxiety in some women, while others sail through it without any problems. The important thing to recognise is that depression is an illness that is genetic in many, even though dormant, and it could flare up at any time into full-blown illness. Anxiety too is probably genetic, and must be accepted as part of your make-up.

Depression can take several forms. The victim may be weepy and withdrawn and without any interest in normal activities, or periods of deep depression may alternate with "mania" – periods of wild excitement and frantic activity, when the brain seems to be racing and overflowing with ideas. Manic-depressive illness has affected some very famous people – Van Gogh being the most well known. In the manic phase great things can be accomplished, if the victim manages to control his rush of ideas and get something down on paper. But in the depressive phase he feels utterly worthless and all his work seems sub-standard. Creative people are often affected by manic-depression, and there is, in fact, some evidence that creativeness may be associated with the gene that carries depression, so that the two are genetically linked. This is a nice theory as it comforts the creative sufferers among us. It does not, however, explain all cases of depression, since not all sufferers are poets or artists.

Another kind of depression that has only been identified in recent years is known as "Seasonal Affective Disorder" or SAD. This is very interesting as it is a purely chemical upset in the body, and it only causes symptoms during the winter.

What happens is this: Deep within the skull there is a tiny gland known as the pineal gland. This gland contains cells which are similar to those in the retina of the eye and are sensitive to light. While the light sensitive function of the pineal gland is only fully developed in lower mammals it seems to play a part in the regulation of the oestrus cycle in many higher mammals, and may function in humans as part of our hormone system and as a regulator of our "biological clocks". The functions of the pineal gland and its sensitivity to light in humans is still not fully understood however, and even "Grays Anatomy" was disappointingly vague about the pineal gland. What is known is that the pineal gland secretes a hormone called melatonin, and abnormally large amounts of this are found in people with SAD. Light suppresses melatonin and with it the symptoms of SAD. What has probably happened is that some people are unable to cope with the low levels of light and short daylength experienced in winter. Human beings remember, are tropical animals and SAD isn't found in the tropics.

The SAD sufferer is perfectly normal during the summer months, but becomes increasingly lethargic and depressed as winter approaches. The sufferer may become so ill that he/she cannot continue working. SAD victims are luckier than most of us because there is a very simple cure – full spectrum light. "Light-bathing" twice a day under this special light will prevent the symptoms entirely.

While SAD is a specific illness in its own right, I believe that most victims of depression suffer from a small degree of this light sensitive malady, and "light-bathing" may be beneficial to all who are prone to "winter blues". SAD or no SAD, the importance of light as an antidote to depression cannot be overestimated. More about this later.

Anxiety can be a separate illness, or it can be mingled with depression. Acute anxiety is a state of perpetual tension and fearfulness. The sufferer cannot calm down, and "nerves" rule his/her life. Often there is a feeling that something terrible is about to happen – a continual dread of some unknown catastrophe. This feeling is caused by the "fight or flight" hormone – adrenalin, and it is the constant flood of adrenalin that gives rise to the classic symptoms of anxiety – palpitations, trembling, muscle tension, and churning of the stomach. In the long term anxiety can lead to many other symptoms such as headaches, stomach ulcers, irritable bowel, even cystitis. All these symptoms lead to more anxiety as the sufferer imagines they are due to disease.

Anxiety sufferers are frequently referred to as "neurotic", by friends and relatives, and they may become hypochondriac, imagining all kinds of serious illnesses. The hypochondriac is desperately trying to explain his or her very real symptoms, so the palpitations become heart attacks, indigestion becomes stomach cancer, and headaches, of course, must be a brain tumour. It never occurs to the sufferer that it is highly unlikely that one person could suffer simultanteously from heart disease, liver failure, bowel cancer, stomach cancer, kidney failure, and a brain tumour. Yet all these diseases may cross his mind as he struggles for an explanation of his symptoms. It doesn't help when exasperated relatives accuse him of "imagining" his symptoms. He is not imagining the symptoms, and they are every bit as real as those caused by disease.

Anxiety is looked upon, even by some doctors, as a "trivial" complaint, hardly worthy of sympathy, and the sufferer is ashamed to admit that his symptoms could be of purely nervous origin. The unfortunate victim will be told to "pull himself together" and "snap out of it", but how can he?

Understanding your illness and accepting it is half the battle, but sympathetic support from friends, relatives, and the family doctor is also necessary. Healthy folk cannot imagine how trivial problems can become blown up out of all proportion to their real importance in the mind of the anxiety sufferer. A healthy person rarely notices his own heartbeat for instance, but a hypochondriac will be aware of every single beat (or, more alarming, the MISSED beats). Even a healthy heart misses beats occasionally, and there are some forms of "arrhythmia" (irregular heartbeats) that are insignificant and harmless. They even affect athletes. True "heart murmurs" are a different thing, and only a doctor can tell if you have a true murmur or a harmless arrythmia.

Pains in the chest may be caused by nothing more serious than a pulled muscle – pulled muscles being common in the anxious – yet the hypochondriac will believe he is having a heart attack. Pains in the stomach are usually due to indigestion and/or wind, and are probably the result of eating too quickly and swallowing air. Air-swallowing (called "wind-sucking" in horses – yes it affects them too) is a common problem in tense and anxious people. Try eating slowly and chew thoroughly before swallowing, mixing food with plenty of saliva. Watch yourself to see that you don't "gulp" air as you swallow.

I had an aunt who was a hypochondriac. So morbidly obsessed with her symptoms was she that every time she visited she would thrust her arm under my nose and say, "Feel my pulse". She also developed an obsession about her weight and always weighed herself on our bathroom scales. One day I hid the scales and she came rushing out of the bathroom in great distress because she was unable to check her weight.

The hypochondriac can try the patience of the best of us, but rather than brush them off irritably, relatives should reassure the sufferer that the symptoms are caused by anxiety. In some cases hypochondria is a cry for help. The sufferer is saying, "Look what this anxiety is doing to me. It's making me ill! Somebody please help me."

If you are a hypochondriac try reasoning with yourself along the following lines, "I've been suffering from these stomach pains for TWENTY YEARS. If it was anything serious I would be dead by now." And, "If I had all the things wrong with me that I imagine I wouldn't even be able to walk! I'd be in intensive care!" Nobody can wave a magic wand over you and make you better. That is something you must do for yourself, and I hope this book will help you.

Depression, anxiety, hypochondria – all these can affect the naturally neurotic individual in varying degrees. Let us look more closely at the depressive personality with a fictional, but typical case.

Mr John Smith is in his forties and has just been made redundant. He feels he has been abandoned on the scrap heap of society long before his time and is too young to retire but too old to start again in a new career. Without a job he feels he has lost identity. He is a "nothing" with nowhere to go and nothing to occupy his time. Weeks drag on into months and he becomes increasingly depressed and apathetic as he fails to find work. His sense of worthlessness grows and he feels he is becoming more than a burden on his family. He sees other men leaving for work in the morning and coming home with fat paypackets at the weekend, but he has nowhere to go, and his benefit money is not enough to support the standard of living he is accustomed to. The four walls close in on him and he gets irritable with everybody.

He lies awake every night, worrying about his future and what he is going to do with his life from now on, and he loses interest in sex. His friends from work have drifted away and he rarely sees any of them. His world seems to be shrinking and there is nothing to break the monotony of the endless, empty days. Nothing seems to give him pleasure anymore, and even his food seems tasteless. He just wants to lie in bed all day. Physically he has no energy and feels constantly tired, even though he is not doing anything. Sometimes he finds himself breaking down and weeping for no obvious reason and is ashamed of himself. He feels it would be better for everyone if he were dead.

You may recognise something of yourself in the above example, and identify with this man. John Smith would probably end up being admitted to hospital, becoming dependent on prescribed drugs, or, if his downward spiral continues he could become an alcoholic (slow suicide) or kill himself.

Now, what about anxiety? Let us look at a typical case of anxiety in the same way. Mrs Jane Smith is married with a teenage son and suffers from acute anxiety. She has always been "nervy" and neurotic, but lately she has got much worse. She spends most of her day as a "couch potato" in front of the television, watching any and every programme. She drinks a lot of coffee and chain-smokes. Forever worrying, she is in a state of constant agitation and tension. Her movements are quick and jerky and she gets trembly when in company, avoiding eye contact. The doctor prescribed Valium for her ages ago and now she is dependent on it. She also needs to take sleeping pills. She no longer bothers about her appearance and has put on a lot of weight. Recently she has begun to suffer from "panick attacks" when out and tries to avoid having to go out. She is troubled with psoriasis and neuralgia, and her life seems to have become one long nightmare of pain and worry.

These two examples of typical cases are amalgams of sufferers I have known, and individual cases may differ from these, but you should be able to recognise at least some of your symptoms and identify with these fictional characters.

The causes of depression and anxiety are many and varied and each case follows its own course. Jane's anxiety, for instance, may evolve into agoraphobia (fear of being in an open space), and John may start drinking heavily and become an alcoholic. A younger "Jane" may develop anorexia nervosa. In all cases, however, there are common bonds. Life loses its sparkle and the world is viewed through grey-coloured glasses. At the same time the mental centre of gravity moves inwards, so that one's primary concern is one's own body, and one's own problems.

Lack of money and grey, miserable surroundings can make anyone unhappy, but a sensitive person can be pushed right over the edge into full-blown nervous breakdown. However, contrary to what most people imagine, a six figure bank balance and a luxurious mansion do not make one immune from depression; psychiatrists are nowhere in more demand than in Hollywood!

It is important to realise this fact, as it is all too easy to blame your problems on lack of money, and believe that winning the pools would erase your troubles forever. It wouldn't, it would just give you new problems. The fault lies within yourself. People can live in the greatest poverty and be happy, while others languish in luxury and are suicidal. The world is always the same, and it is you who changes. If you don't believe me, consider the following scenario:

One morning you drag yourself out of bed feeling depressed as usual. There are overdue bills to be paid, and no money to pay them. Your refrigerator is empty, but you are too tired to be bothered, and cannot bring yourself to trail up that High Street one more time. Everything can just go to hell! Then the postman calls and a slim brown envelope is pushed through your letterbox. "Oh no. Not another bill," you cry, and you dread opening it. But this letter is different.

When you open it you find a letter inside informing you that you have scooped the jackpot on "ERNIE" and a quarter of a million pounds is on its way to you. How do you think you feel now? Do you still feel tired? No, you are off up that High Street like a streak of lightning, a big soppy grin on your face, and you buy champagne and flowers and feel as though you are dancing on air. Suddenly the whole world is brighter, and everything seems to be rejoicing with you. Even the rain is beautiful! Make no mistake – the world has not really changed at all – it is *you* who has changed. Now wouldn't it be wonderful if you could feel as though you've come up on ERNIE now, without any change in your circumstances? "Never," you say. Well we will see . . .

Your world can be full of rainbows and sunshine and music and laughter, or it can be a bleak place filled with twilight and tears. It all depends on you. "But how can I feel happy when my world is coming apart?" I hear you say, "Look at me! I've got nothing. I am worthless. Everything is against me." Yes, so it may seem in your present state of mind. But hopefully, if you follow the advice in this book to the letter, and really give it a chance, things will change. As your state of mind changes things will look brighter, I promise you.

The problem with depression is that it pulls you into a downward spiral. Depression causes negative thinking, which generates more depression, and more negative thinking and so on. If you drop a stone into a pond, you see ripples moving outwards until they break upon the edge. Although you cannot see it happening, everything you do or say is like that stone being dropped into still water. If you think negative thoughts then negative vibrations are sent out. And what happens when the ripples in the pond reach the edge? They are reflected back again. In the same way, your negative vibrations will come back to you and make your life more miserable than ever. This, my friend, is the Law of Karma and there is no getting away from it. Whatever you send out you will get back; you reap exactly what you have sown. The Law of Karma is beautifully presented in the great Indian epic, "The Ramayana", with the following lines:

"Deeds we do in life, Kausalya, be they bitter, be they sweet,
Bring their fruit and retribution, rich reward or suffering meet.

Heedless child is he, Kausalya, in his fate who does not scan
Retribution of his karma, sequence of a mighty plan!"

Karma is so important in understanding the causes of our suffering that I have devoted a whole chapter to it. There is little point in tackling the symptoms of your illness without an understanding of its cause.

The Anti-Depression Plan works at all levels, both spiritual and physical, rooting out and destroying everything that could be feeding the Black Beast. It is a kind of exorcism if you like, a purging of mind and body. Such a purging is bound to be painful at times, and you must be prepared for the pain. People tend to become so used to their depression that it can be quite frightening when the depression is taken away. It has become a kind of crutch to them. If life's pressures get too much for you, you can fall back on your depression, run to earth and lick your wounds. Without your illness to fall back on you are going to have to face up to those pressures. That is the price of happiness, but I'm sure you will agree it is worth it.

By the very nature of their illness, depressed people lack courage, or believe they lack courage. They feel defeated and beaten down by life, and have no strength left to raise themselves up. Thoughts and feelings become wholly negative. Listen to the things you think and say. Keep a diary of your thoughts and you will be shocked by its negativity. How many times do you use the words, "No", and "Never" and "Nothing"? Are your thoughts full of bitterness and anger? Do you repeatedly say "I hate" and "I loathe"? Is "I wish I were dead" one of your favourite sentences? Are the words "Wonderful" and "Lovely" and "Beautiful" almost non-existent in your vocabulary? Do you write with ferocity and aggression or is your writing weak and shaky?

When I first read my own diary as if I was somebody else I was horrified at the hate and bitterness it contained. And everything was negative. "Nothing good ever happens to me" was a favourite phrase. So full of envy, jealousy and resentment was I that it is hardly surprising I had a miserable life. Stand back from yourself and look at yourself through the eyes of a stranger.

I know what you're going to say now. "Is he one of those Positive Thinking gurus? I don't want any of that. My life is falling apart for Chrissakes. How can I be anything BUT negative?"

There are a vast number of books and tapes on Positive Thinking available now, but they only work if you believe in them. And that is where most people fail. Because when you are in the depths of despair it is well-nigh impossible to believe that everything is going to start coming up roses. It is absurd to expect someone who is struggling to manage on a paltry welfare cheque to go around saying "I am rich" all the time. They only have to look around them to see it isn't true. I will not expect you to be THAT positive – yet. That will only become possible later, when you have got yourself out of the dark pit you are now in and you begin to feel better and see some results. Once on the road to recovery you will begin to have positive thoughts spontaneously, and that's when to study and practise all this Positive Thinking! For now, your chief priority is stopping your downward spiral of negativity, depression, more negativity and deeper depression, and that is all I expect from you. The Plan will help you to do it.

CHAPTER TWO

UNDERSTANDING KARMA

"WHY IS THERE so much suffering in the world?" "If there is a compassionate God, why does he permit such suffering?" How often have you heard these cries of despair? "WHY!?" we scream in anguish. "Why?" has echoed down the ages, from the Great Plague to the two world wars – and from the Holocaust to the latest plane crash. It is a question churches shrug off with an unconvincing, "It must be God's will".

Many people are lucky enough to sail through life without ever experiencing any hardship or suffering, but others have to flounder from one problem to the next and life seems to be nothing but pain and disappointment and broken dreams. In our deepest depressions none of this seems fair, and God is seen as hostile and uncaring. Thomas Hood was very moved by the suffering of poor seamstresses in 1843 and he wrote "The Song of the Shirt". We will all recognise the despair in these lines:

"O! Men with Sisters dear!
O! Men with Mothers and Wives!
It is not linen you're wearing out,
But human creatures' lives!
Stitch – stitch – stitch
In poverty, hunger, and dirt,
Sewing at once, with a double thread,
A Shroud as well as a shirt.

But why do I talk of Death,
That Phantom of grisly bone?
I hardly fear his terrible shape,
It seems so like my own –
It seems so like my own,
Because of the fasts I keep,
Oh! God! that bread should be so dear,
And flesh and blood so cheap!"

Although this was written over a hundred years ago, this same despair is felt by many people today. It does not say a lot for progress that the last two lines are still quite valid!

Suffering is timeless, and the question "why?" will always be asked, sometimes silently, sometimes cried aloud to an unheeding sky. "Why did God allow this to happen?" and "why has this happened to me?"

Religion is supposed to answer such questions, but the Judeo-Christian tradition has never had a satisfactory answer. It is necessary to venture outside the Judeo-Christian faith to find the answers. The Hindu religion is one of the oldest in the world. And in India, its birthplace, suffering and death are a fact of life. But Hindus see suffering in a very different way. This is because they believe in KARMA. Karma and SAMSARA (the belief in reincarnation) can do much to make suffering more tolerable. Modern esoteric teachings recognise the Law of Karma and it is generally accepted by occultists everywhere.

Karma is usually described as "Action and Reaction" or "Cause and Effect" and is popularly compared to "destiny". Each person lives according to his or her own karma, and everything in the material world has its karma. When you are born you carry over a karmic balance from your previous lives – and this may affect the circumstances of your birth and the events immediately afterwards. From childhood onwards however, fresh karma is created and is added to the karmic balance.

Everything you do, say, or think, creates a ripple in the ether, and this in turn creates karma. If you do bad things you create bad karma, but this does not mean that suffering is necessarily the result of bad karma in the past; there may be other reasons. Higher Beings known as the Lords of Karma may give us ordeals to go through as part of our learning process. These are not meant to break us but to strengthen us. Karma demands responsibility, because whatever you do to others will eventually come back to you; if you hurt somebody you will have to suffer for it. But the worst karma comes from misusing the subtle forces of the Universe.

In a well-known and extremely reputable occult magazine I counted ten advertisements for books and talismans designed to help you influence others. "Secrets of Mind Domination" one said, and it continued, "Here are the amazing secrets of mental influence the masters do not want you to know . . . how about using it to make you master of any man or woman you choose . . . to make people melt to your desire . . . how to seize control of people using a special gaze!"

Anybody attempting to use such powers would face the wrath of the Lords of Karma, and would pay heavily for the privilege. I recall a letter to the above-mentioned magazine about this. The writer was baffled by the ignorance of people who can be taken in by such dangerous rubbish. But people never learn. If you remember the example of a stone dropped into a pool you will have an idea of how karma works. But there is one important difference. Karma multiplies the "rebound" effect, so that what you get back is greater than what you have sent out. It will be seen that evil thoughts and actions will bring you more suffering than that inflicted on your victim. This is what we call a "Karmic Debt". And like all debts, karmic debts, once created, must be paid. You may escape payment for a time, but sooner or later your karma will catch up with you.

Everything you have ever done or said, has created karmic credit or karmic debt. Dr Douglas Baker in his book "Karmic Laws" says: "He who is the original actor in any trail of events has the most responsibility and karma to bear, good and bad though it may be. Nature will extract retribution to the utmost for what has been done and will reward and compensate in the same sort of manner.'"

If a person is desperate for money, they may foolishly go to a "loan shark". The loan shark will give the money willingly, and the foolish person will go home marvelling at the ease with which they were able to obtain it. Only later, when it is time to repay the loan, will the unfortunate person discover that the interest is 200 per cent. And when he cannot meet the repayments, that is when the loan shark turns nasty. If you ask for a "psychic loan" be sure you can handle the repayments.

Karma is terrifying in its ruthlessness, but it is also beautiful. For suddenly you will see that life is no longer "unfair". Everything evens up eventually. The man who lives in a palace in this life, probably lived in a slum during his past life, or he may find himself in the slum during his next life! Nobody is particularly favoured, although it may appear so at times. The child who dies at three years old may live to be ninety in the next life, so he isn't being "robbed of life".

The concept of "sin" is a misguided understanding of karma. Jesus himself was fully aware of karmic law, or he would not have placed such emphasis on the virtues of love and compassion. The problem Christ faced was that He was trying to teach very simple people some highly complex and esoteric things, and it was left to these people to interpret what He said.

There is a lot of misunderstanding about karma in the West. Karma is not direct "Divine Retribution", nor is it "Fate". It is never final, or fixed, and is ongoing. Each day you create fresh karma for your future, and each day you reap the karma you have sown in previous days. Some people reject karma because they don't like the idea of events being "predestined", and feel, quite wrongly, that karma is fatalistic. The truth is that karma is always open to change, so long as you know how to go about it. If you have lived contrary to karmic law you will have to pay the price, and this price has to be accepted. But you can begin this very minute working off your bad karma and building up karmic credit rather than karmic debt. The best way to earn karmic credit is by practising "AHIMSA" – "harmlessness", and giving of yourself to others. The Ten Commandments are mostly karmic laws, so by keeping the Ten Commandments you obey karmic law too. But karmic law demands more from you than this if you wish to pay off all your karmic debts.

One thing you must never do is interfere with another person's progress in life, and even some supposedly devout Christians are guilty of this. Evangelists who believe they are "saving" people may actually be leading them AWAY from the path. The kind of religious leader who whips up a frenzy of religious fervour in his followers, establishes communes, and separates young people from their families, while at the same time raking in all the money he can lay his hands on to "fund his church" – he is actually serving the devil, not God, and he is breaking the Law of the God he professes to worship. No-one has the right to possess the soul of another person, even in the name of religion.

In business, riding rough-shod over colleagues with never a care, like a real life J. R. Ewing, is asking for trouble. While everyone needs to be assertive, and a certain amount of competition is necessary and healthy, your gains should never result in harm to others. Harming anyone for the purpose of personal gain creates very bad karma!

We have all encountered those hardened monsters who seem to live without any regard for others. All that matters is their own happiness and their own progress. The "five H man" (Hell How He Hates Himself) who is so wrapped up in his own over-inflated ego that he isn't even AWARE of the sufferings of others, is riding for a karmic fall.

Does all this mean that desiring success and wealth is wrong? Well no – not if the Laws of Karma are obeyed. There are two types of rich and successful persons; those who take all they can get for their own selfish pleasures and to hell with the rest of the world, and those who use their wealth, and the privileges it provides, to be of service to others. Money in itself is not evil. What matters is how money IS USED.

What would you do if you won a million pounds on the pools? If your answer is, "I'd spend, spend, spend!" then you would find your wealth short-lived and unfulfilling. Karma gives and karma can take away if a gift is being misused. Sudden wealth doesn't always bring happiness; wealth can be just as much a trial as poverty.

I have a friend who has experienced both sudden and substantial wealth, and poverty. He became rich overnight when his pop group shot to Number One in the charts. They all had a whale of a time – until the taxman caught up with them. They had to pay almost half of what they earned to the taxman, and if they had spent it all they would have been in deep trouble. He refers to those days as "an experience" but would't like to go through it again. He told me that money can give you material comfort, but it never gives you guaranteed happiness. You can be just as lonely and unhappy in a palace as in a slum, and we have all heard of wealthy people who are anything but content with their lives.

My pop singer friend has left "the good life" behind him, and is quite happy being an ordinary guy. He has taken a job as a signalman because he loves trains, and he spends his holidays in a little cottage in Scotland. He's no longer rich or famous, but he is happy.

Wealth and fame need to be handled correctly if they are to last. A lady who knows how to handle her wealth is Brigitte Bardot. Once the world's most beautiful and desired woman, she now devotes her life, her home, and a large chunk of her income to animals. She works tirelessly for the rights of animals, using her position as a public figure to draw attention to her cause. She even visited baby seals on the ice to help in the campaign against the cruel culling of seal pups. This kind of selfless devotion towards helpless creatures will not pass unnoticed by the Lords of Karma. They can reward as well as punish.

Bob Geldof is another celebrity who devotes his life to helping others, and Jimmy Saville yet another. Both seem to know instinctively how to be wealthy and successful and yet remain in harmony with karmic law. People who are generous and give of themselves will never be poor. This may sound strange but it is true. Al Koran in his wonderful book "Bring out the Magic in your Mind" says "Tithing fulfils the law of increase" and elaborates, "I have never known anyone to tithe properly, and not receive a thousand times more than they have given."

Al Koran advises us to give a tenth of our money to charity, and I have made a point of doing this as ten per cent of your income doesn't add up to much and can easily be spared. I would, of course, remember to give away ten per cent of my prize money if I won the pools or came up on Ernie. It is very important to repay the Lords of Karma if you have been granted such a blessing.

Hollywood stars who have fulfilled every material desire are often unhappy because they feel something is missing in their lives. What has happened is that they have neglected the spiritual needs that every soul has. The soul needs to see advancement also, and if the soul is neglected there is an imbalance. Many stars become "born again Christians" to fulfil their spiritual needs, but this is taking things to a rather fanatical extreme. All that is required is a little spiritual awareness. Recognise the presence of God in your life and love Him. Learn how to meditate and tune into the peace that lies within you, and say a prayer every day.

Every home should have a shrine of some sort – a tiny corner where one can escape the noise and pressures of modern life. Somewhere you can find peace and sanctuary at any time of the day and night. At its simplest, this can be a low table on which is kept a candle, some fresh flowers, and perhaps a Bible or other holy book. You can add an incense burner if you like, icons or pictures of holy subjects, and perhaps crystals used for healing.

If you have the space and the money, you can turn a whole room into your own private sanctuary. A sanctuary can be created to suit any religion, from Christian to Hindu to Pagan. Nowadays there are specialist shops that contain many beautiful objects that would grace one's sanctuary – candles of all colours and types, New Age music tapes, incense, oils, statuettes, pictures and posters, crystals, even pyramids!

We have talked a lot about good and bad karma, but how do you decide if something is creating bad karma? The rule is this – if it is harmless than it is karmaless, but if it harms anyone, even indirectly, then it will create bad karma. By harming "anyone" we are referring not just to human beings but to EVERY LIVING THING. This brings us to some difficult issues – such as meat-eating.

Hindus, who understand and accept the doctrine of karma, in daily life, do not eat meat. Jains, another religious group in India, go even further than this. Their respect for life is such that they even wear masks to prevent their breathing in and accidentally killing an insect. They also have to watch every step they take lest they should step on some insect in their path! This high regard for life is most admirable, but quite impossible for most of us. We should, however, go as far as we possibly can towards respecting the sanctity of life.

If the carnivores of the world hope to take comfort from the fact that killing for food is "necessary" they are fooling themselves, for as far as human beings are concerned killing for food is not necessary, since we can (and many millions already do) live without eating meat. A true carnivore, such as a tiger or a wolf, or even your dog and cat, can kill without incurring karmic debt, because their role in the karma of the Earth is to maintain the balance between carnivore and herbivore. Human beings however, are not carnivores, and meat eating is an adopted habit. There are very few circumstances where it would be karmaless for a human being to take the life of another animal. Perhaps if you were dying of hunger in an Arctic wasteland – but certainly not in an average town where there are plenty of alternatives to choose from.

You cannot escape the fact that every time you sit down to a meal of meat you are adding to your karmic debts. Whether you are prepared to accept this debt is up to you, but if you already have a heavy karmic debt and a lot of bad karma to work off it is foolish to add to it! The best way to begin working off a karmic debt is to take a vow of harmlessness. This means giving up eating meat. You have to accept that harmlessness and compassion are incompatible with the horrors of the slaughterhouse.

If you want to become vegetarian do it gradually, and find out how to eat a healthy diet without meat. It is not enough just to leave the meat off the plate and eat your vegetables. The body needs protein. Now there is a lot of nonsense surrounding vegetarianism. Firstly, a vegetarian diet does NOT have to consist of nothing more exciting than salads, more salads and nut cutlets. You can eat almost the same foods you ate before, except that they contain beans or textured vegetable protein instead of meat.

Another myth is that a vegetarian diet will leave you somehow "undernourished". (Even doctors can fall for this one, especially if they were trained in the days of "First Class Protein" and "Second Class Protein".) The body needs protein, but it doesn't really matter where that protein comes from so long as it is complete. Men may worry about becoming "wimps". This is another myth! Look at the elephant, the rhinocerous, the gorilla, the bull and the stallion – all vegetarians. (If you don't like the term "vegetarian", why not call yourself a "herbivore" instead? MUCH more macho!)

The importance of harmlessness and compassion cannot be over-emphasized. All-encompassing love for ALL living things is your aim. When you first attain this state of mind it is a wonderful feeling, and you will know instinctively that it is "right". You will feel that you have raised yourself above the rest of humanity, and are nearer to God. All encompassing love is not easy, and it will prove rather fleeting at first, but those moments are to be treasured. They give you a glimpse of what it feels like to be God.

God is capable only of love. He is Light and Love, no more, no less. But SUCH Light, and SUCH Love! Retribution and punishment is left to the Lords of Karma, but they don't dish out trials and tribulations out of anger, spite or sadism. They are incapable of such emotions; totally logical Beings, who see only logic, learning and rightness.

When people have been dealt a cruel blow by life they try to blame somebody. Often they blame God, when He is not to blame. In coping with a bereavement – perhaps as a result of an accident – it is difficult to avoid bitterness. "Why did it have to be HIM?" "It's not fair!" The Lords of Karma, in their wisdom, know that death is meaningless. It is merely a transition between two lives. And if you loved someone dearly in this life, it is quite possible that you will meet them again in the next. Sometimes two "soulmates" will be together through several lives. Even whole groups of people have been reincarnated together.

Krishna comforted Arjuna on the battlefield with these words:

"Thy tears are for those beyond tears; and are thy words words of wisdom?
The wise grieve not for those who live; and they grieve not for those who die – for life and death shall pass away.

"Because we all have been for all time: I, and thou, and those kings of men. And we all shall be for all time, we all for ever and ever . . .

"He is never born, and he never dies. He is in Eternity: he is for evermore. Never-born and eternal, beyond times gone or to come, he does not die when the body dies . . .

"As a man leaves an old garment and puts on one that is new, the Spirit leaves his mortal body and then puts on one that is new . . .

"For all things born in truth must die, and out of death in truth comes life. Face to face with what must be, cease thou from sorrow."
(The Bhagavad Gita 2: 11,1 12, 20, 22 & 27)

While I was in hospital a few years ago I met a nursing sister who was a real tyrant! No-one came closer to the fictional "Nurse Diesel" in the Mel Brookes film "High Anxiety". At first I hated her, then one day she spotted me reading The Bhagavad Gita and was interested. She sat down and poured out her soul to me, telling me how much she grieved for her dead brother, and how bitter she was about everything. I realised that this woman was really very nice at heart, but bitterness had soured her and made her the way she was. She didn't believe in reincarnation, but wanted to believe in it, and kept saying how wonderful it would be if it were true. "But it IS true!" I said, and I showed her the verses I have quoted above. She then confided in me that she had always felt her grand-daughter was uncannily like the brother she had lost and could she possibly be a reincarnation of him? I smiled. "There's no reason why not," I said.

That woman left my room a much nicer person, and had at last found comfort. The bitterness and resentment had gone and she had come to terms with her brother's death at last.

Now you may be unable to accept reincarnation, and the only reason I have gone into it here is that from personal experience I know that it can give an immense amount of comfort to the bereaved. However you come to terms with death, realise that reincarnation or no reincarnation, we all go on "for ever and ever". There is a time for mourning and a time when mourning must end. Life has to go on.

Ultimately we are all responsible for our own karma, and we must accept that responsibility. We are given ordeals in order that we learn from them and aid our soul's development. If we fail to learn the lessons our suffering will continue – sometimes going on for life after life. What is gained from a terrible ordeal is often more than what was suffered, but we fail to see these gains. Remember, each incarnation is a new beginning. With each new life we have the opportunity to start afresh and correct the mistakes we made in previous lives.

If you still need convincing, look to the scriptures of your religion. Although karma may not be referred to as such, it is clearly understood and its laws are included in the scriptures of the world's main religions.

Whatever you have suffered in the past, and whatever you have to suffer now, the first step is to accept your situation without bitterness or resentment. This is by no means easy but it is the only way you can change your karma. Accept your karma and try to see what it is teaching you, and what good you can get out of it. Surrender to karma and give yourself to God. With surrender comes peace at last.

"Love worketh no ill to his neighbour: therefore love is the fulfilling of the law." (Romans 13:10)

"Be not deceived; God is not mocked: for whatsoever a man soweth, that shall he also reap." (Galatians 6:7)

"To those who do what is good, goodness and increase! . . . But, as for those who have earned ill, the reward of evil is the like thereof." (The Koran)

"But great is the man who, free from attachments, and with a mind ruling its powers in harmony, works on the path of Karma Yoga, the path of consecrated action." (The Bhagavad Gita 3:7)

CHAPTER THREE

THE EIGHT POINT
ANTI-DEPRESSION PLAN

NOW THAT YOU UNDERSTAND your illness and the karma that lies behind it, it is time to take the first steps towards recovery. You are going to need determination and courage to take your Black Beast by the horns, but hopefully, by now, you will be ready and willing to do something. You have been wallowing in negativity long enough – now is your chance to take your life in your hands and turn it around. Be bold, be positive, and give it all you've got. Behind you there is nothing but darkness and misery. That is familiar to you and feels "safe", but do you really want to remain in such a sorry state for the rest of your life? Before you there is, or should be, a faint glimmer of light – the promise of better days.

Imagine you are on a gigantic ladder. The base of the ladder is planted firmly in the darkness where quicksands wait to swallow you up. The first rung is the twilight world of the lower planes – a dismal place where lost and broken souls congregate, trying to find a way out. Many suicides end up here, and here they will stay until they understand the karma that brought them to such a tragic situation and they resign themselves to their karma, accept it, and make a definite decision to work their way up the ladder, however difficult it may seem to be.

The next rung is that of hopelessness, where the soul teeters on the brink of a fall. Here suicide is contemplated and the world is a very dark place indeed. Each rung from here on up represents a slightly more positive atitude and by the middle of the ladder the darkness is being left behind and your world becomes a much brighter place. Finally we reach the very top of the ladder, which vanishes into the blinding white light of the Highest Planes. Only a small percentage of people ever make it to the top. Equally, only a few unfortunate souls slip right down to the bottom. Most of us are somewhere in between. Where are you on the Ladder of Life? By pinpointing your position on this imaginary ladder, which has nine rungs, the middle one representing Hope, you can see exactly how far you have to climb and you can use it to monitor your progress.

All you have to do is ascend the ladder one step at a time. Forget the top rung which represents Complete Fulfilment, just concentrate on the rung above the one you are on now. You can linger on a rung for a while if you wish, but the important thing is to keep moving upwards and never allow yourself to slip down. If something should come along that knocks you down, such as a bereavement, accident, or financial crisis, scramble up again as soon as you possibly can. Set time limits on periods of depression and misery and don't let them take over your life.

We all have good days and bad days, and these ups and downs of life cannot be avoided, but do not let the bad days rob you of happiness. I call these really awful days my "Black Fridays". When a Black Friday comes along, make a bargain with yourself. Tell yourself you can wallow in misery to your heart's content, so long as it is just for that one day! Tomorrow you will put it all behind you, pick yourself up, and carry on. During a Black Friday cry as much as you like, let everything go hang, yell, scream, and be as negative as you wish. But the next day you must wipe away the tears and carry on climbing that ladder. This is the One Day Rule, and it is the only way to deal with situations of temporary crisis.

In the case of a really severe blow, such as a bereavement, one day will not be sufficient. You may require a month or more to get over it. But set a time limit. Tell yourself you will mourn for exactly two months, or six months, or even a year, but when that time is over you will be done with mourning, because you have your own life to think about. There is no need to forget about the person (or pet) you have lost – you never forget them. But when the time limit is up you will return to all your normal activities and do away with any outward manifestations of grief, for life must go on and you have your own destiny to fulfil.

The anniversary of a death is a good time to finish mourning and move on to a new life. On that day you can quietly let your loved one go, and turn towards your own future.

I think I should say something here about the British tendency to keep a "stiff upper lip" in times of emotional crisis. Emotions are good and natural, and act like a safety valve, relieving otherwise dangerous internal tensions. During a crisis allow yourself to express emotion and never suppress it. It always amazes me how funeral guests say a widow is being "very brave" when she doesn't cry, as if it was commendable! Contrast the behaviour of British widows with those in countries such as Spain or Italy or India where grief is expressed openly. Never bottle up your emotions. Weep if you wish, there is no shame in it. Expressing emotion is normal.

The British male has a tough time of it compared to the men in other countries. Boys are discouraged from expressing emotion and crying is "cissy". It is all a lot of nonsense. Latin males, who are generally considered to be very "macho" weep openly, and nobody thinks any less of them for it. Crying is good for you. Not only does it act as a safety valve, releasing a lot of harmful tension, but tears carry away toxins from the body. A good weep will make you feel miles better. If you are male and shy about tears you can always shut yourself in the bathroom or bedroom and cry in private. But DO cry when you feel the need.

Adrenalin is the anxiety hormone, and it is adrenalin that causes the symptoms of acute anxiety. Bottled up tension, fear, or anger, can be very damaging to your body. Stress and tension that are allowed to simmer within will eat away at your stomach causing ulcers, affect the functioning of your bowels causing irritable bowel syndrome, and can lead to headaches, neck pain, back pain and eventual arthritis. In fact bottled up tension can lead to innumerable ills.

The purpose of adrenalin is to prepare your body for "fight or flight", but of course, in modern society it is just not possible to react to threatening situations by fighting or fleeing. So the outflowing of adrenalin becomes self-destructive.

There are ways in which you can release this tension however, in a manner that satisfies the fight or flight instinct and stops the flow of adrenalin. Instead of bottling up your anger and stewing inwardly, release it – not on your boss or spouse but on something inanimate and indestructable. Have a cushion or a punchbag handy, and when you need to get rid of some "aggro" let rip on it. The cushion or punchbag cannot be harmed by your blows and you will feel a lot better afterwards, having released your anger.

In situations where you are very nervous, and your natural instinct is to flee, go jogging. Take a sprint round the block. Again, you're doing what nature intended but in a totally harmless manner. And once you have released the pent up emotions the production of adrenalin will cease and leave you feeling much calmer.

By using the methods above you will be able to reduce your level of tension to a minimum and it will not then act as an obstacle when you try to ascend the Ladder of Life.

Instead of a ladder, you may prefer to imagine yourself climbing a mountain. You are starting up a long and winding path that leads to the summit, and there are nine "base camps" along the way. On your climb you will encounter many difficulties. Sheer, almost impossible faces, violent storms, slippery slopes . . . but you keep going because you know you must. When the summit is in sight things will seem easier because you can see you are making progress and you'll be encouraged.

The Eight Point Anti-Depression Plan should not be tackled half-heartedly. Go into it with a will to win and beat your illness into the ground where it belongs. You may need to wait, and meditate on it for a while, searching your soul for the incentive to begin. But if you really want to get better, sooner or later you will wake up one morning and say to yourself: "I can't go on like this for the rest of my life. If there is a chance of recovery I have to take it. After all I have everything to gain and nothing to lose." When that day comes, don't let the Black Beast talk you out of it, begin the Plan immediately!

No guarantee can be made for the effectiveness of the Plan, as it all depends on YOU. But if you genuinely want to get better (even though you cannot see how that is going to come about and you follow the Eight Point Plan to the letter, you will notice some relief. Nothing will happen overnight, so you must be patient and stick with it. Do not be discouraged if you don't have instant results – it takes time to change a lifestyle and a way of thinking into something more positive. The important thing to remember is that however small your progress appears to be, you are doing something about your depression. And that is a very positive thing! Perhaps it is the first positive thing you have done in years.

Let the Plan become a new way of life and you will find it is a powerful weapon against your illness. You will still get depressed sometimes, even very depressed, but with the One Day Rule this won't last, and you will be able to pull yourself out of it and smile again.

One fact you must come to terms with – nobody can wave a magic wand over you and dispel the black clouds that hang over you. You have to do that. The cure must come from within. So let's set the wheels in motion.

The eight parts of the Plan are:

1. DIET	5. CONTACT WITH NATURE
2. LIGHT AND COLOUR	6. MEDITATION AND MUSIC
3. AIR AND EXERCISE	7. ACTIVE MENTAL EXERCISE
4. POSITIVE THOUGHT	8. SPIRITUAL SUPPORT

CHAPTER FOUR

DIET

A DEPRESSED PERSON tends to either overeat or lose interest in food. Both disorders will have a detrimental effect on the general health and hence on the mental health. Make sure your body is properly nourished by eating a healthy wholefood diet. Boil-in-the-bag snacks and chips with everything just won't do; you are what you eat.

When people describe themselves as feeling "alive" or "dead" they are closer to the mark than they realise. There is literally more than meets the eye to the food we eat.

Kirlian photography is a technique that has been developed to show the normally invisible fields of energy surrounding all living things. Living things, as seen in a Kirlian photograph, really do "glow" with health.

All living things have an energy, referred to variously as the "life force", the "chi" or "prana", and the occult teaching is that prana descends to Earth in sunlight and is absorbed by plants and animals. Kirlian photographs startlingly reveal this energy, and it appears as a brilliant white light mingled with electric blue. It is the energy that forms the "aura' that clairvoyants can see, and it extends beyond the outline of the body. The brilliance of the aura varies, and Kirlian photography shows with chilling clarity how it turns darker and fades away, eventually disappearing, as fruit, for example, rots.

This prana is the very stuff of life, and the less you have of it, the less alive you are. Stress, pain, ill-health, all can deplete your prana, and if this deficiency is not made up your physical health will suffer. When people say a dying person is "fading" they are right. The aura of a dying person grows dim.

Depletion of prana can result in numerous physical effects. The immune system fails to work properly and you suffer endless colds, 'flu and sore throats. Allergies may appear. Gradually all the ills that plague the anxious and depressed manifest themselves, and the (literal) lack of energy results in perpetual tiredness.

Life force or prana is brightest in raw, freshly harvested, organically grown fruit and vegetables, and least in cooked, stored and chemically grown foods. I remember seeing two Kirlian photographs of a cabbage, taken before and after cooking. Before cooking the cabbage was brilliant with white and blue light, and had a healthy aura. After cooking, however, there was practically no light at all. The cabbage was dead! From this it will be seen that if vegetables are eaten in the fresh, raw state the life force will pass into your own energy field and add to it. If foods are eaten cooked and "dead" they will contribute nothing to your life force, and many of the vitamins will also have been destroyed.

Human beings, like all other living things need to take in vital energy every day. When this is depleted, ill health results. Whenever we complain of "having no energy" it may be that our level of prana really is low, and our subconscious, aware of this fact, is simply stating what it knows to be true.

The human being is the only animal that cooks its food. Every other species eats fresh raw foods all the time. Cooking can therefore be said to be unnatural. The closer an animal gets to eating the foods that are natural to it – those it evolved to eat – the healthier it will be. Zoos have proved this time and time again. Many of the ills that afflict human beings are caused by our unnatural diet. Nowadays, not only do we cook food; we freeze it, can it, process it, add chemicals and colourings to it, strip it of fibre, and add abnormally large quantities of salt and sugar to it.

Some of the "foods" eaten today hardly qualify as foods at all – they are totally artificial chemical concoctions that can do our bodies nothing but harm. One chemical colouring – tartrazine – is proven to produce adverse effects in many people, particularly children. A friend of mine had a young child who was hyperactive and quite impossible to control after he had been given a tartrazine-loaded "orange squash" at playschool. When she complained and got the playschool to stop giving the children this artificial orange squash her child's behaviour changed dramatically.

When you consider how powerful a tiny pill containing a drug can be, and you learn that the average person consumes something like a teaspoon of artificial additives every day, it is really very frightening. What are all these chemicals doing to us? Not only do we take in chemicals directly in our own food, but chemicals such as preservatives and colourings are also added to animal feed, so that your meat will also be full of them!

It is difficult to avoid all artificial chemicals, but fortunately the food manufacturers are waking up to the fact that people do not want their food contaminated in this way, and each day there are more and more additive-free products on the supermarket shelves. Long may this trend continue!

Now, while the ideal human diet would consist of fresh, raw, additive-free foods of a predominantly vegetarian nature, few of us can manage to stick to such a diet, especially once the cold weather sets in. So compromises have to be made, but our aim should be to keep AS NEAR AS POSSIBLE to the ideal diet. By eating the ideal diet, and avoiding all artificial chemicals, we will keep our bodies healthy. And tip top physical health is a great help in the battle against depression and anxiety.

The ideal diet will be vegetarian or almost vegetarian, but not vegan – dairy produce is, I think, necessary for several reasons. Skimmed or semi-skimmed milk is an excellent source of calcium, and calcium, apart from building strong bones, is also essential for the proper functioning of the muscles and nerves. Deficiency of calcium in horses leads to tetany and in cattle to milk fever. A drop in blood calcium may also lead to tetany in humans. Stiffness of the muscles and muscular spasms are the main symptoms of tetany.

If you don't want to give up meat altogether, then reduce your intake of it until you are eating it only once or twice a week. And eat GOOD meat – not processed meats. Beware of sausages that contain lots of colourings and preservatives, and processed meat rolls. Eat your vegetables in as fresh and natural a state as possible, and include lots of fruit in your diet.

To maintain a healthy level of prana in our bodies there must be at least as much coming in as that being lost. Sadly, like their bank balances, most people are perpetually "overdrawn". Life force is lost daily and if it is never made up you will never enjoy perfect health. Stress, worry, shock, anxiety – all deplete prana at an alarming rate – it is the loss of prana, remember, that makes you feel tired when you are suffering from "nerves".

Fresh prana is obtained from sunlight (which is why everyone feels good on a sunny day), the air you breathe, and from food and water. Everyone should try to get a little sun each day, but people who live and work in smog-ridden cities may hardly see the sun, and they depend on air, food, and water for their daily intake of prana. So what are they eating? I think they would get a nasty shock if they could see a Kirlian photograph of the average business lunch. Hamburgers, white bread rolls, fat sodden chips, all these are "dead" foods and contain no prana at all. Such foods fill you up, they taste nice, and they may give you some protein and carbohydrate, but the vital life force is missing. If most of your food is "dead", it is no wonder you feel tired and run down.

So what do we eat instead? The ideal lunch would be a salad with some potato and cheese or something similar, and when I say salad, I do not mean the ubiquitous lettuce, tomato and cucumber.

I will never forget a trip I made to London Zoo one very hot summer's day. I was passing round the back of the mammal house when I chanced to look through a window, and saw what appeared to be a kitchen where people were preparing salads. But oh, what salads! Shredded cabbage, sliced carrot, beetroot (raw), chopped apples, celery, a handful of nuts and some chopped boiled egg. My mouth watered at the sight and I immediately looked for the entrance to the restaurant so that I could have one of these super-salads.

But a shock awaited me. What I had seen was the kitchen of the mammal house, and those wonderful salads were for the animals only! I'll give you three guesses as to what was on offer in the human canteen. Chips and sausage, chips and egg, chips and beans, chips and chips. I could not stomach any of the greasy mess they put in front of me, and longed to go back to the mammal house where there was some proper food.

This "Mammal House Salad" has become one of my specialities now, and it is just bursting with vitamins. Throw convention to the wind, and chuck in any kind of vegetable you fancy, all raw. Add fruit such as chopped apple and banana, and perhaps chopped boiled potato. Then add protein in the form of nuts, eggs, or a slice of tofu. You will never want an ordinary salad again.

There is so much that can be eaten raw, yet people never think of trying such things as zucchini (courgette), beetroot, turnip, peas, beans (broad), and mushrooms raw. I think they would have a pleasant surprise if they did. Only cook what you must cook, and then cook for as short a time as possible, the only exception being meat which should be very well cooked.

Everyone who has a garden, even if it is just three foot square, should cultivate it and grow their own vegetables. Aim to become as self-sufficient in vegetables as possible. If your garden is too small, see if you can rent an allotment, or come to an arrangement with somebody who has a big garden they can no longer manage alone. It is nothing short of criminal to let good growing land go to waste. Apart from the fact that gardening is a most excellent therapy, there is nothing to beat home grown produce, and with your own plot you can harvest vegetables just moments before serving them when they are still alive and full of energy.

If you do not have a garden, and cannot get the use of one, you can still grow some of your own food. "Sprouted seeds" are all the rage now, and can be bought in health shops and garden shops everywhere. Mung beans, adzuki beans, chick peas, fenugreek and alfalfa, can all be sprouted on your kitchen windowsill. Just put a handful of beans into a wide necked jar (soak mung and adzuki beans overnight first), cover the top with muslin kept in place with an elastic band, and rinse out the jar once or preferably twice a day, until the shoots have grown to the required length. Then you can use them either as they are or stir-fried with rice. If you are a keen sprouter you can buy a special seed sprouting device that consists of tiered plastic trays. This is better than the jar method. All the sprouted seeds are packed with vitamins and minerals, and sometimes protein too, and they are very high in life force, prana. With the three or four tier design of sprouter you can grow a different "crop" on each level.

Mustard and cress can also be grown on a windowsill. Cress is extremely nutritious, and can also be sown in rows in the vegetable garden for spring and summer crops, and harvested with scissors.

It is important that all white flour products are replaced with wholegrain alternatives, for these contain the B vitamins, so essential for combating stress. No more white sliced bread I'm afraid! Pasta too can now be bought as wholewheat, instead of white. Sugar should be reduced to the absolute minimum, but there is no need to exclude it from the diet altogether. The same goes for salt. Where possible use honey as a sweetener, for honey is very good for you, and helps calm the nerves.

Bran should be a regular part of your diet, although this should not be your only source of "roughage". An excellent remedy for an upset stomach, constipation, and/or flatulence and colic is a "bran mash". Put two to four tablespoons of bran into a bowl, mix with pinhead oatmeal, wheatgerm, buckwheat, and any other grain you fancy, pour on a dessertspoon of black treacle or molasses, and then mix to a gruel with hot milk. Eat this last thing at night before retiring. It is a gentle and natural laxative and gives your insides a good "spring clean". Laxative drugs should never be necessary, and if they are then something is wrong with your diet.

Keeping the bowels regular is vital, especially in depression. Toxins from impacted faeces will poison your whole system and increase your depression. Drinking plenty of water is helpful in keeping the bowels open, as well as flushing out your kidneys and keeping your whole body healthy. It is surprising how dehydrated many people are, and this is made worse by excessive consumption of very salty snacks. Have at least one good long drink of water every day, and always drink after eating anything salty.

If your water is excessively polluted or full of fluoride and other contaminants it is better to drink fruit juices and non-alcoholic beer, or buy bottled water. Avoid entirely those highly coloured sugary concoctions that pass as "lemonade" but have never seen a lemon or anything else that is natural.

Cut down all sweet, fatty, stodgy foods and replace them with fruit and vegetables and natural snacks. Never use lard or suet. Butter is all right, but don't eat too much of it for health reasons.

Meat is the ultimate "dead" food. In fact, not only does it contribute nothing to your life force, but it will actually deplete it during its digestion. This is one of the reasons you feel lethargic and sleepy after a big meat dinner. If possible then, change to a vegetarian or semi-vegetarian diet. This is more important for the depressed – anxiety sufferers are probably better on a diet that includes a small amount of meat.

In addition to foods being "alive" or "dead", they are also "positive" and "negative". The polarity of a food can be discovered by using a pendulum. Every pendulum user has his or her own method, but with me a clockwise rotation means positive, and an anti-clockwise rotation is negative.

It can be very revealing to test a variety of foods in this way. For optimum health there should be a perfect balance of positive and negative foods, but, since depressed people have too much negative energy, they should eat more positive than negative foods. As most negative foods are also fattening this keeps the weight in check as an added bonus. The most positive foods are; root ginger, bean sprouts, fresh green vegetables, fresh fruit, carrots, onions and many spices. Negative foods are milk, pasta, potatoes, oils and fats, and all flour products.

We are now getting into the more esoteric principles of nutrition, and you may be quite unfamiliar with these. Ancient "Ayurvedic" medicine recognises the three natural qualities of "Rajas" (fire/active), "Sattva" (light/unifying), and "Tamas" (darkness/passive).

Rajas food is defined as acid, sharp, salty, or dry; while Tamas foods are stale, tasteless, or rotten. In Ayurvedic medicine people are classified according to which of these three principles is dominant in their make-up. Thus, fiery Rajas people (typical natives of Aries or Leo for instance) like Rajas foods (plenty of chillies in the curry). Tamas people on the other hand, like Tamas foods (dull, boring people, generally like dull, boring foods).

If you see Rajas as positive, Sattva as neutral, and Tamas as negative, you will realise that to obtain the desired state of Sattva, a balance of Rajas and Tamas foods must be eaten at every meal. When the positive and negative energies are in harmony within the body, it enjoys perfect health. This is also the theory behind the ancient Chinese art of acupuncture.

If all this mixing and matching of food sounds too complicated for you, don't worry. Once you learn which foods are positive and which are negative, balancing them is easy. Potatoes, for instance, if eaten on their own are negative, so you should eat something positive with them – a green vegetable, carrots, spices or ginger.

Indians use a variety of spices, and not only do they liven up otherwise bland (and negative) foods, but they stimulate the digestive juices, and enhance the flavour of food. Potatoes fried with some spices and a little bit of root ginger, together with some onion and garlic are a tasty, cheap, and perfectly balanced dish. Not all spices are hot – in fact most of them are not hot at all. The hot one is the chilli – fresh, dried, or powdered. Use chillies with caution if you're not accustomed to them, and remove the seeds from fresh chillies if you prefer them not so hot. Depressed people, particularly if they have lost interest in food, should eat spices. They are very positive!

If you have digestive problems go easy on the chillies or leave them out altogether, but spices such as coriander, cumin, turmeric, paprika, cinnamon, and fenugreek are good for the digestion, and are recommended. A little spice makes your meals more interesting, and they stimulate the appetite.

Before we leave the esoteric principles of food, it is useful to know that foods can be classified according to which element rules them. This little bit of trivia would be unimportant if it was not for the fact that depressed people have too much of the "earth" element in their bodies, and this excess earth element can be counteracted by eating a lot of "air" foods, since air opposes earth. Crazy as this may sound in theory, it works.

The characteristics of the earth element are inactivity, heaviness, dullness, darkness, and decay. The depressed person feels heavy and lethargic, they are mentally dull and unstimulated by life, and they are attracted to surroundings that "suit" their unhappy mood. How many depressed people do you know who take a morbid delight in visiting graveyards, or sitting in dismal rooms with curtains drawn and wilted flowers rotting in a vase on the table? The leaden quality of the earth element dominates their lives, and depresses them still further.

What we are trying to do here is to change all this, and bring air and light into the sufferer's life. So introduce the air element in every possible way. Let us eat "air" foods, surround ourselves with light and "airy" colours, listen to "air" music, and take daily exercise in the fresh air. The qualities of air are weightlessness, expansiveness, brightness, and vitality, and these are the very qualities the depressed person lacks.

Imagine your depression as a black beast, a sort of invisible vampire or gremlin. It cannot abide light, air and colour. In the same way that garlic repels vampires, light, air, and colour repels the black beast of depression. Attack your black beast from all sides and from all levels, inside and out. Drive it from your body by making the body utterly hostile to it. Fill your body and your home with all the things the black beast hates. Don't FEED your depression, FIGHT it.

As far as food is concerned eat as much as you can of the "air" foods; bean sprouts, coconut (fresh), rice, honey, tofu (beancurd), lychees, citrus fruits, berry fruits, peppermints and mint flavoured foods.

You will find that these foods "lift" your mood and make you feel energetic, while heavy, negative foods make you feel worse. Food should energize you, not slow you down. It should excite your tastebuds and make you feel good. Explore the wonderful world of food and expand your gastronomic horizons. Sample exotic fruits, cook dishes from other countries and other cultures.

A farmer I once knew visited my house. He amazed me when he pointed at an avocado pear ripening in my fruit bowl and said, "What's that thing?" "An avocado," I said. "Never seen one of those before," he said, "What do you do with it?" As I enthused about the virtues of the humble avocado I knew it was a waste of time. He would never try one for himself. He would go home to the same old mince and potatoes. His diet was so restricted that he would have to eat the same things several times a week, which must be *extremely* uninteresting. Don't limit yourself in this way. Find out all you can about the exotic fruits and vegetables you see in your greengrocer's or supermarket and buy them. Soon they will no longer be "exotic" to you, but quite ordinary. After all, at one time the tomato and the potato were exotic foreign foods!

If you are one of the "good plain food" variety, you don't know what you are missing. The exquisite rose flavour of the lychee, the golden sweetness of the mango, the fragrance of a papaya, the chestnut-like flavour of a sweet potato; try them all. Stimulate your tastebuds and your imagination.

"Hold on," I hear you saying, "How can I afford to buy all these exotic fruits on my income?" Well you can if you want to, it depends how you look at it. A mango or a papaya costs less than a packet of cigarettes, yet you will happily waste money on a packet of cigarettes, won't you? Buy the fruit instead and give yourself a treat. Then something like the avocado, which is so rich in nutrients as to be considered a complete meal in itself, makes a very cheap lunch.

You don't have to buy cookbooks to find out how to use all these new foods either. You can get them from the library and copy out the recipes you want to keep. Do not go through life with blinkers on, expand your consciousness beyond what is ordinary and familiar. Depression thrives on sameness and hates new experiences!

Now, no matter how well you eat, nervous tension and depression will deplete your body's reserves of vitamins, minerals and the all important trace elements. Nervous illness is extremely debilitating, and unless you can keep to a diet of raw fruit and vegetables three times a day, every day, you cannot get all the nutrients you need from your food.

If there is a small hole in the bottom of a bucket, you will never be able to fill it right up, because the water will run out as fast as you pour it in. This is what nervous illness does to your body, and it uses up nutrients faster than they are taken in, leaving you with various deficiencies. In addition to this, the body requires more than the normal amount of some nutrients while you are suffering from nervous illness, in particular the B vitamins and certain minerals. A supplement, therefore, is strongly recommended.

Get the best multi-vitamin and mineral supplement you can find, with a large selection of vitamins, minerals, and trace elements listed on the label, and make sure it has good quantities of the B vitamins in it. In addition, take one tablet or capsule of Red Korean Ginseng every day. Ginseng has the most remarkable properties and can be looked upon as a "plug" that stops up the hole in your "bucket". It insulates the body against the ravages of stress and makes you stronger and better able to cope. It has now become quite expensive, but is worth its weight in gold, so don't let the price put you off.

Honey is another essential "supplement". Barbara Cartland sings the praises of honey, and although she may, at times, exaggerate its virtues, it is undoubtedly a wonderful food with many uses. Try it as a sweetener in a cup of chamomile or lime blossom tea, and spread on toast with your breakfast. Or stir it into freshly made natural yoghurt. Honey and ginseng taken daily can work wonders!

Once you have established your new diet it will become second nature to you, and you will grow to love it. While sticking to the diet is vital, especially at first, the occasional "wicked" treat, such as a sticky bun, does not matter. After all who can feel depressed when they're sinking their teeth into a Black Forest gateau?

CHAPTER FIVE

LIGHT AND COLOUR

LIGHT IS LIFE. Darkness is everywhere associated with death. Drive out the darkness from your home and let the sunshine in. Depression hates sunshine and cannot survive in a bright, airy, sunny environment. Never put up with dismal surroundings, or dark and depressing colours. These things feed your depression.

Look around you right now. Is the room bright and cheerful, or is it dull and miserable? Is there dark wallpaper with large, claustrophobic patterns on it? Is the paintwork grubby and yellow with age? Are the colours drab – slime green, bridge grey, manure brown, sick sepia, and sour cream? (Colours beloved of councils everywhere!) Perhaps you have fallen for the subtle persuasion of fashion, and you have decorated the walls in grey or beige with black furniture? Are you unwittingly creating a perfect home for the Black Beast?

Starting right now, get rid of everything that looks dismal or depressing, because you cannot hope to recover from your illness with surroundings that are drab, claustrophobic, or miserable. Redecorate if necessary in bright, happy colours. Emulsion paint is cheaper and easier than wallpaper and looks great. You can give each room of your house a different colour scheme. There is one rule in choosing colours – the smaller the room the lighter the colour. In very small rooms you cannot go wrong with white – it reflects the maximum amount of light and gives a feeling of spaciousness.

My bedroom is lemon yellow and white with curtains of tangerine. I used to have a blue colour scheme in my bedroom, then I realised that this colour was a perfect match for my "blue" moods. In an emergency I had to put up some spare tangerine curtains and I was astonished to find that this colour had an energizing effect on me and merely looking at it made me feel happy! So I said, "To hell with convention. If I like orange and yellow, I'll darn well have orange and yellow," and I did. Of course, everyone is different, and you may loathe yellow. In that case you must find which colour cheers you up and base your bedroom colour scheme on that. Quietly ignore the current craze for dark and dingy colours. Your recovery is more important than fashion. Colour schemes based on grey, beige, off-white, dingy purple and brown are just asking for trouble, and I think black and red are also bad. Choose light pastel shades; sunny, summery colours, and brilliant white. Soften a white room with lots of green plants, and touches of gold here and there.

Well chosen pictures can enhance the feeling of brightness and cheerfulness and chase away gloom. As I write this I am looking at a large poster of a beautiful tropical beach, and I have a similar picture, in oils, hanging over the fireplace. Even in the depths of winter I can see blue skies, white sands, and the translucent turquoise of a tropical ocean. Choose "positive" pictures like this – pictures that depict happy scenes and beautiful summery landscapes. Never hang a dismal picture on your wall. Your pictures should feature blue skies, green meadows, turquoise (not grey) oceans, colourful flowers, birds, butterflies, young animals and children. You may not have given a thought to the pictures on your walls before, but now you must. It is more important than you think, because you are looking at these pictures several times a day, every day, imprinting them on your subconscious. You want to imprint the right things on your subconscious, not things that will feed your depression.

If you have difficulty finding suitable pictures, why not try your hand at painting some? It was because I could not find or afford the right kind of paintings that I tried it myself, and a new hobby was born. One favourite picture is hanging on my wall right now. It is of a little Mediterranean village set at the foot of rolling hills. Beyond it there is a shining blue sea, merging on the horizon with the azure of the sky. I look at this scene and I can almost feel the hot sun, and smell the fresh tang of the sea, mingled with scents of myrtle and citrus groves.

Cover your walls with bright, happy pictures. Posters, paintings, pictures from old calendars, anything you find uplifting, inspiring and beautiful. Start a scrap book of happy pictures. Collect pictures from magazines and holiday brochures and fill your scrap book with these. Then you can browse through it whenever you want cheering up.

Light and darkness are opposites, so drive away the dark by letting in as much light as possible. Take down heavy curtains and dingy blinds, and never keep blinds down all day. More than anything else, light has the power to banish depression. There is a sacred quality to light, for God Himself is a Being of Light. God is "Limitless Light". No evil can exist in the glare of intense natural light.

All angels and saints are shown with a halo of light, and heaven itself is filled with light. People who have had "Near Death Experiences" describe how they pass through a dark tunnel and emerge into light. Sometimes a Being of Light greets them, standing by a Portal of Light. This "holy" light is no ordinary light – it is so bright that it would blind the mortal eye.

In the Bhagavad Gita, Krishna describes the appearance of God thus: "If the light of a thousand suns suddenly arose in the sky, that splendour might be compared to the radiance of the Supreme Spirit." (11:12) Can you imagine the light of a thousand suns shining down upon you? This is what it would be like to stand in the Divine Light. The Bible says that the very first thing God did when He created the Earth was to make light. "And God said, let there be light: and there was light." (Genesis 1:3)

Light is Divine, and the Divine is light. Wherever there is light, there is the presence of the Divine. Whenever you are frightened or threatened by evil visualise an enormous sphere of blinding white light, shining down upon you and filling your body with its radiance. Bask in the Divine Light and darkness cannot harm you.

Just fifteen minutes of sunlight a day is enough to stop the symptoms of SAD – Seasonal Affective Disorder. Sunshine fills you with life force – prana, makes vitamin D to strengthen your bones, and stimulates the pineal gland, so keeping the blues at bay. Nowadays people are discouraged from sunbathing because of the small risk of skin cancer, but sunlight is vital to health and you must not shut yourself away from it altogether. Even if you spend just fifteen minutes in the sun, it will help you. Few people think of sunbathing in winter, but it really does help to banish the winter blues! Wrap up warmly and sit with your eyes closed and your face raised to the sun for fifteen to thirty minutes every day the sun is shining.

Make the most of the light that comes into your home by capturing it and amplifying it. Prismatic crystals hung in a window will catch the rays of the sun and throw rainbows of coloured light all round the room. Tap the crystal gently with your finger and you will fill your room with dancing rainbows. I cannot think of a nicer present for someone who is ill or bed-ridden. These "sun crystals" can be seen in "New Age" or occult shops. Some novelty shops also stock them. Have as many as you can afford, and in as many windows as possible.

Glass and lead crystal ornaments placed on a sunny windowsill will catch sunlight and give out the pure white light that is so reminiscent of the Divine. Even better are earth crystals themselves. Clusters of quartz, amethyst, and many others can now be bought in New Age, occult, or special crystal shops. These are not just beautiful ornaments – they have definite healing properties. In fact, crystals have really come into their own during the last few years, and there are many books on crystal healing.

Find out about crystals, buy them, and use them. Crystals can be purchased as clusters, as points, and even mounted so that they can be worn as jewellery. The theory of crystal healing is simple. Our bodies contain subtle electro-magnetic forces. Crystals, especially quartz, have the ability to regulate these forces. Millions of watches and alarm clocks use this principle and contain quartz crystals that keep them accurate.

There are other ways of using light for healing. One company has marketed a solar cell enclosed in a medallion that is worn around the neck. A tiny electric charge is produced when light falls on the solar cell, and this passes into your body through the chain. Electricity has long been used to accelerate healing in medicine and is even used on racehorses. The makers of the "Solar Energizer" claim that it makes you feel more active and healthy and that it can cure many minor medical problems. Whether it really works or not is up to every user to decide, but it is a fascinating idea, and another way of harnessing the power of light.

Kirlian photography shows the human aura as a halo of light. When we are healthy this halo of light is brilliant and complete (you quite literally "glow" with health), but when we are ill the colours of the aura become darker and tears or shadows may appear. If you feel as though you have a "dark cloud" hanging over you, you probably have – in your aura. Illness and mental suffering batters the aura and damages it, weakening it and leaving you open to all kinds of harmful forces.

In order to strengthen the aura, carry out this simple "light visualisation" exercise every day: Sit cross-legged on the floor and face a source of light. This light must be natural and sunlight is by far the best, but daylight or even candle-light will do. Close your eyes and allow yourself to fully relax, retreating into the silence of your own mind. Now begin to breathe slowly and deeply, keeping to a regular rhythm of inspiration, holding the breath, then exhalation. Visualise an intense white light shining down on you from above from an imaginary sun. As you inhale see this light being drawn into your body and filling every part of it; then as you hold your breath, see your aura glowing brightly all around you, making your whole body shine and scintillate. Finally, as you exhale, see the darkness within you passing down and out through the soles of your feet. At each inhalation you are charging your aura with prana, drawing in light through every pore. Later on we will combine this exercise with a breathing exercise that will make you feel wonderful.

Are you agoraphobic? Do you suffer from "panic attacks" while you are out and feel uncomfortably exposed and vulnerable? If so, there is a very simple exercise you can do anywhere that will help you overcome this fear. Imagine you are inside a transparent, but quite solid, plastic bubble. Visualise this snapping shut around you and shutting out the world. The bubble is so thick nothing can penetrate it and within it you are completely safe.

If you find yourself in an unpleasant situation where you want to put a stronger barrier between you and the people around you, make this bubble opaque or turn it into solid lead. Charge the bubble with white light, seeing it glowing all round you like a force field. You might prefer to imagine a force field rather than a plastic bubble, especially if you are a Sci-Fi fan. Practise projecting your own personal force field until you can do it instantly and it becomes real to you.

You can use a similar technique to place a circle of protection around your bed, or even your house if you feel frightened and vulnerable. If flying or travelling in trains or buses scares you, imagine the plane or the vehicle surrounded by a pink force field. Mentally draw a circle of protection around it, and then place a symbol of protection over it – a cross or a pentagram. Don't underestimate the power of this exercise. It is more than imagination, for you really do create a circle of protection – a "ley" or line of magnetic force in the Earth's magnetic field.

To protect your bed or your house, you will need to draw a circle. Starting on the East side, point your finger and visualise a beam of brilliant electric blue light streaming from it like a laser beam. Trace a line where you want it, all around the place you are trying to protect, seeing the line shining like a trace left by a Firework Night sparkler. Whe it is complete, see the circle as a line of white fire. You can draw signs at the four points of the compass now – crosses or pentagrams. Be sure to draw the circle in a clockwise direction though.

This is how witches draw magic circles and done properly it is a very powerful barrier. In case you are saying, "Hey, I don't want to use witchcraft," it is also the way a priest consecrates holy water or communion wine. The power of magic can be used for good and in the name of God, and the clergy use it all the time without realising what they are doing. Whether it is a Priest tracing the sign of the cross over a goblet of wine, or a witch drawing a magic circle, the result is the same. An invisible but persistent impression is inscribed on the ether, and this lasts until sunrise or sunset, when it must be renewed.

Light is holy. Light is life. Prana or life force appears as tiny sparks of brilliant white light. (In the next chapter I will tell you how to see this.)

Get as much light into your life as possible, and drive off the darkness that surrounds you. When you do the Light Visualisation Technique, imagine you are basking in the light of a thousand suns. No darkness can exist under this barrage of light, and the Black Beast of depression will be driven away. Allow yourself to soar on the white wings of light and experience joy, if only for a short while. Gradually, as you change your environment, the Black Beast will relinquish his hold on you, and set you free.

CHAPTER SIX

AIR AND EXERCISE

IT MAY BE OLD HAT, but it's true; plenty of fresh air is vital to your physical and mental well-being. In modern centrally heated environments, fresh air is becoming a rare thing, and people have to work in the most appalling atmospheres. A growing problem is so called; "Sick Building Syndrome". Some eminent scientists are unable to explain why certain buildings suffer from this and cause a higher than normal incidence of headaches, lethargy, stomach upsets and other minor ailments in the people who have to work in these buildings. The cause is simple – lack of fresh air. In "sick" buildings, windows are sealed so they can never be opened, and air is pumped through an air conditioning system that is often full of moulds, dust, and stagnant water. No wonder people get ill!

When I worked on a farm we raised about a hundred beef calves in a purpose-built calf house every winter. This was warm and roomy, and calves were loose on deep straw – a perfect environment you might think. But the calves began to suffer epidemics of pneumonia and other diseases in spite of our putting the ventilation fans up to full speed. Experts came down to try and locate the problem but could not find anything wrong. The answer was discovered more or less by accident – we left the back doors slightly open. Day and night, in all but the stormiest weather those doors were left ajar and there was a dramatic drop in the incidence of pneumonia. Fresh air had cured our "sick calf house".

Now I am not saying human beings should try to live with a window open all the time. Most of us would find that very uncomfortable, apart from the effect it would have on our heating bills; but no building should ever be made where the internal environment is closed off from that outside, and where windows cannot be opened to let in fresh air on mild or warm days. If you work in such a building complain to the management and demand that fresh air be admitted to the building.

Homes can be "sick" as well as offices. Make a rule that you will air every room in your house at least once a day – preferably leaving windows open for an hour or two. In cold weather you can do this while you have lunch, or are in another room, switching off heating if necessary beforehand, so as not to waste it. Get out into the open air every day too, even if it is only for a very short time. Invalids and disabled people should be taken out each day, and on warm days allowed to sit in the sun.

It appals me the way hospitals are kept permanently stuffy and airless, and patients are never allowed to venture outside. If you try to open your window in hospital, sure as hell somebody will come along and slam it shut! While patients must be kept warm, it beats me why there should be such an aversion to fresh air even in the summertime. And patients who have only minor complaints, or are nearly ready to go home, should be allowed to go outside (if there is somewhere to go other than the car park). How lovely it would be if every hospital had a garden where patients could go to sit on warm sunny days, and they could even do some of the weeding. But fresh air and the healing power of growing plants has very low priority in hospitals – a great pity.

There is more to fresh air than just air. Another cause of Sick Building Syndrome is lack of "prana" as well as lack of oxygen. Prana is the very stuff of life and pure, clean air is loaded with it. It is the energy equivalent of oxygen, but does not exist on the physical plane – it comes from the higher planes. The reason why people feel particularly invigorated on sunny mountain meadows is because of the very high concentration of both prana and negative ions in such places, as well as plenty of fresh air.

Prana is the energy of life – the stuff that quickens a body into life. You can pump oxygen into a corpse, but oxygen alone will not bring it back to life. What is missing is the prana. Prana is what flows along the "meridians" of acupuncture (although the Chinese call it by another name – Ch'i). It is what makes spirits luminous, and is what we are referring to when we say someone is "glowing" with health. Air without prana is not enough, which is why closed environments are so very unhealthy. Stale air is not only low in oxygen but is low in prana too, and also in ions. Prana comes down to earth in sunlight and fills the atmosphere. It is taken up by living things, and when they die it is returned to the atmosphere. Because prana comes directly from the sun, there is much more around on sunny days than on dull days, and concentrations are also higher at other times – morning rather than afternoon, spring rather than autumn. Prana is greatest in a mountain meadow on a spring morning, and least in a coal mine on a winter afternoon!

Never live in a stuffy, airless environment, and never tolerate it at work. Nowadays you can buy "ionizers" to improve the quality of the air you breathe, but remember that prana – life force – is even more vital.

If you need to see prana to believe in it, here is an experiment you can do. Take a brisk walk to the top of a hill on a clear, sunny morning, preferably in spring or summer. If there isn't a suitable hill near you, then find a balcony or wide-opened window above ground level, and out of the city. A beach by the sea is also a good place.

Stand with your face raised to the sky and begin to inhale deeply, breathing through the mouth as well as the nose, with your mouth slightly open so that you are drawing in air through your teeth with an audible hiss. If you are standing before an open window, it is better to kneel, but don't sit back on your heels.

Breathe deeply between ten and fourteen times (make it six or seven to begin with if you are elderly or unfit). When you begin to feel light-headed, *stop*. Now look up into the sky, breathing normally. Refocus your eyes so that you are looking at a point just a few feet in front of you. Look AT the air, not through it. What you should see are hundreds of little sparks of light, swirling around like champagne bubbles. They move very rapidly in all directions, and you will find that the deeper you breathe the clearer they become. What you are seeing are particles of prana. You may think it is a trick of the eye, but you will find you no longer see them as easily indoors, or in a stuffy airless environment, or even at the wrong time of year. (There is less prana reaching us in winter as well as less sunlight.)

The slight light-headedness produced by this exercise is due to overbreathing, and will not harm you provided you stop as soon as you feel it. To continue past this point could make you faint, so do be careful. Any dizziness can be counteracted by covering nose and mouth with your hands for a few breaths. You will soon discover you can control your breathing so that you can carry out the exercise above with no risk whatsoever and you will find it quite "intoxicating".

Once you have mastered the breathing, complete the exercise by raising your arms as you inhale, slowly and gracefully, like the wings of a bird, until the tips of the fingers meet over your head, and your arms form an inverted V. Then lower your arms slowly as you exhale. I call this "prana breathing" and it is a wonderfully invigorating exercise.

When you are practising the prana breathing regularly once a day, you can, if you want, combine it with the "Light Visualisation" exercise given in the last chapter. See yourself surrounded by shining white light and breathing in white light through every pore as you inhale. This exercise – the Prana Breathing together with the Light Visualisation, will have the most miraculous effect on your mood. It will make you feel wonderful, and the "high" can last for quite a while afterwards. You can make the exercise even more effective by combining it with suitably "uplifting" and expansive music – more about that later.

The first time you do prana breathing and see prana, you will be amazed. To realise that you are seeing the very essence of life will fill you with awe. It is the energy from these minute specks of light that gives your aura its luminosity, and it is prana that is the difference between life and death.

If you cannot get to a hilltop every day, you can do the exercise by a widely opened window. You won't always see the prana but it does not matter. Once you have seen it you know it is there. Do prana breathing every day, preferably in the morning or at noon, and always outdoors or by an open window. You only need to do the exercise once. Only repeat it if you are young, fit, and you know what you are doing.

Deep, slow, regular breathing should be practised until it becomes second nature. When people are tense or nervous their breathing becomes fast and jerky, with perhaps a "double lift" occurring during inspiration. By controlling your breathing, and ensuring that you always breathe with the abdomen, not the chest, you will calm yourself down.

In very tense situations you can calm yourself by practising the yogic art of "Pranayama" – breath control. Place your right (or left if you are left handed) hand over your nose so that your first three fingers rest on the top of the nose, and the thumb and little finger are pressing on each nostril. Now, using your little finger to close off the left nostril, breathe in only through the right, making it slow and deep. When your lungs are fully inflated, close the right nostril using the thumb, and hold the breath as long as you find it comfortable, then release the right nostril and breathe out again. Do the same on the left side. Keep breathing like this – first through the right nostril, then through the left, as long as you wish, and you will find that if you concentrate on your breathing as you do, it will remove all nervousness and tension. Finish the exercise with an inhalation through the right nostril.

Pranayama can be combined with the Light Visualisation exercise as well, and you can take it a stage further by doing the following: breathe in through the right nostril as before, but this time count how long it takes you to fully inhale. Hold the breath for the same count, then breathe out, this time through the opposite nostril and keeping to the same count. As an example, if you inhale for a count of eight through the right nostril, you will then hold your breath for a count of eight, and exhale through the left nostril to a count of eight. This is a form of meditation.

A variation of prana breathing and pranayama is "air meditation". This is, like prana breathing, a miraculous mood lifter. Choose a bright sunny morning in spring or summer, and kneel before a widely opened window. Do prana breathing first, then read the following out load, breathing deeply and visualising what you are reading:

"Air of pure air, menthol fresh! I am the white light of the morning! I am the high morning sun, the blinding light of life! My breath is the breath of life. My wild winds blow away all cares, all melancholy, all disease! I am the wild, unfettered breath of freedom! The whiter than white! The lighter than light!

"I am the white dove flying high and free, far up in the azure sky, soaring through the blue infinity. I flow freely on the rafts of the wind, all fragrant with myrtle and citrus tree. Purest white am I, as the feathers of a dove, close to the sun. I am the white light of the morning, the whiter than white! My prana rushes in through every pore, filling the body with life and light.

"My soul reaches for the high unclouded sun, and I soar ever upward on white wings of light! I taste the salt breezes of the sea, the clover fields, the groves of lemons, the fragrance of myrtle. Sunshine and the light of the dawn revolve in my portal.

"My soul is the white dove, soaring high in the blue, crystal stratosphere, carried along by the wind! Winds of ecstasy and freedom, lighter blue to virgin white! The high stratosphere's blinding light! Air of pure air, blow away all my cares!"

After several days or weeks you will have learned most of this by heart and you can recite the words from memory. It is not necessary to use these exact words, so long as the meaning is the same.

Visualise yourself soaring as a bird above a sparkling turquoise ocean. Below you is a small village of white-washed cottages with red shingle roofs. Nearby there is a grove of lemon trees, or perhaps a field of lavender. Visualise whatever you want, so long as it symbolises freshness, lightness and sunshine. Rolling fields of flowers going down to the sea, seabirds by a rocky coastline – it does not matter, so long as it fits the words above, for these are carefully chosen to give you the feeling of the air element. You are meditating on the air element, because air is opposite to earth, and depression and unhappiness is ruled by the earth element.

If you do the prana breathing and the air meditation, I can guarantee that you will feel light, happy, and full of energy afterwards. It is impossible to stay depressed while doing these exercises. By doing this you can get as high on pure clean air as on any drug, and how much better it is than life-destroying drugs. It costs you nothing, it is safe and easy, and it can be done by anyone.

One final exercise you can do, which is particularly useful if you feel yourself to be "under a dark cloud" is the "Jet Stream Visualisation".

The Jet Streams are very strong winds that blow in the upper atmosphere; they can reach four hundred miles an hour. Visualise yourself being raised up into the Jet Stream, and feel the howling gale blowing away all your darkness, leaving you radiant with clean, white light. Combine this with prana breathing, or/and listen to suitable music. In all these exercises see yourself breathing in not just fresh air, but white light.

Fresh air is so important that you should get outside at least once a day. When you are very depressed, you become lethargic, and it's all too easy to be a "couch potato" all day, but this will not help you get better. Set yourself a realistic exercise target. It is no use saying, "I'm going to jog two miles every day," when you know only too well that you will never keep it up! Start close to home and say, "I am going to take a walk round the garden twice a day." If you do not have a garden say, "I am going to walk to the end of the street every day." And do it. Come rain or shine you will still take your daily walk.

If you have a garden, it is amazing how much changes in a day. Fresh flowers open, shoots appear overnight, buds burst, you may see a butterfly, or be enchanged by the songs of birds. There's always something new to interest you. If there is a park near you, take your daily walk in the park, and take a real interest in what you see. Can you name all the flowers and trees you see? What birds or butterflies do you see? And have you ever thought of going out into your garden at night? Night air can be very refreshing, and in the summer months you may meet a hedgehog sniffing around, whereas in winter the stars are a sight to behold.

While walking is a perfectly acceptable form of mild exercise, you should try to do something a little more vigorous if you can. Jogging suits some people, cycling others, but both are very public and many sufferers from nerves and depression are rather too introverted to go out exercising in the streets. In this case you can do the next best thing, which is running on the spot. Open the windows wide and run as if you were on a moving treadmill, increasing or decreasing the speed as you wish. After a few minutes running there is a "rush" of energy that lifts your spirits and makes you feel strong and fit and able to do anything. The high from a good run can last several hours.

To make the exercise harder, lift your legs higher. To make it even harder, do a "piaffe". The piaffe is an exercise done by dressage horses, and they are trained to do it by being harnessed between two poles. You will have to imagine the poles. The idea is to keep your body absolutely still from the hips up and move only your legs in a rhythmic "prancing" motion. This is harder to do than running and gives the legs a tremendous work-out.

Weightlifting is good for the arms and shoulders, but it is not necessary to deadlift four hundred pounds. Any weight will do; a barbell or dumbell if you can afford them, a bag full of rocks or a piece of lead. Like jogging or running, weightlifting gives you a "rush" and makes you feel on top of the world. If you have allowed yourself to "go to pieces" through depression, getting in trim again will improve your self-esteem no end. A rubber ball is a good and cheap exerciser for the arms. There are many different ways you can squeeze and compress the ball to exercise different sets of muscles.

Yoga is an excellent form of exercise, especially for those who are tense and anxious. All too often it is pushed in the West as a sort of slimming programme for woman, when in actual fact it is a form of moving mediation, and its real purpose is to balance and regulate the flow of prana within the body. T'ai chi is the Chinese form of yoga, and serves the same purpose. You do not have to go to classes if you don't want to. You can get books from the library that will teach you the basic yoga postures. Do learn yoga, for it is unsurpassed as a means of stretching and relaxing tensed and aching muscles, and as it balances your internal energies as well, it is of great value to anyone who feels beaten down by life. The easiest postures of yoga can be done by anyone – you don't have to tie yourself in knots.

Whatever you choose to do, you must exercise every day, and carry out the breathing exercises. Force yourself to do something, no matter how depressed or tired you feel. Depression hates exercise and fresh air and I promise you that you will feel better for it!

CHAPTER SEVEN

POSITIVE THOUGHT

DEPRESSED PEOPLE ARE highly negative. They think negatively, speak negatively, and act negatively. As explained earlier, this negativity leads one into a downward spiral which can only end in suicide – the ultimate negative action. You need to do some self-analysis to see how harmful this negativity is. Do you ever find yourself thinking or saying the following negative things?

"Life is a joke," "Nobody loves me," "I'm so ugly and stupid!" "I can't do ANYTHING!" "I'm no use," "There must be a curse on me – all that ever happens to me is bad!", "I NEVER feel well these days," "I don't care anymore!" "To hell with everything!" "Nothing good ever happens to me." "I've got nothing to live for!"

This list could go on and on. Does it sound familiar? How many times have you said these things? I will hazard a guess that you have even had negative thoughts about this book. ("Who is he kidding? Nothing can make ME feel better! I can't be bothered doing all these things anyway – it is too much effort.")

A depressed friend of mine once said, "No, don't talk to me about positive thinking. I don't believe in that anymore!" I still haven't convinced her that negative thinking is actually making her situation worse, and is deepening her depression. "But how can I think positive when everything's against me?" I hear you scream at me, "It's just not possible. I CAN'T think positive!" (There is that word again – CAN'T – the most negative word in the dictionary!)

There is a quotation by Langbridge in "A Cluster of Quiet Thoughts" that I always keep in the back of my mind. It is:

"Two men look out through the same bars:
One sees the mud, and one the stars."

There are always two ways of looking at something – a positive way and a negative way. The depressed person always chooses the negative –

he sees only mud and never the stars. To him there ARE no stars! The sky is permanently overcast with black thunderclouds. So what can he do to change this way of thinking? Well he can start by acknowledging that the stars might be there, that the storm will pass and the skies will clear. That is all – no more, no less. Do you think you can manage to make this small step towards positive thinking? Take one step up the Ladder of Life and say to yourself, "Well, maybe things are not so bad after all – maybe these troubles will pass and everything will be all right."

Many of the books on positive thinking expect too much too soon. You cannot realistically expect someone who has not got a penny to their name and who is up to the eyeballs in debt to put on a big grin and say "I am rich! I am wealthy and successful!" The evidence of their poverty is all around them and it is impossible to deny it. What you can expect from that person is a compromise. They can say, "Things are bad now, but they will get better. I will start by doing this . . . and then that . . . and I will never get myself into a mess like this again!"

The old saying, "When one door closes another opens" is true. You may not see how things can possibly get better, but if you allow yourself to believe they might, they will. It is one of the laws of nature that when something ends, something else begins. Death is followed by birth. Nothing remains in one state forever. Hindus see God as manifesting Himself in three different forms – Brahma, the Creator; Vishnu, the Preserver; and Siva, the Destroyer. Siva is depicted in countless sculptures and paintings as dancing within a ring of fire. He also dances in graveyards and on battlefields. Why on earth would a god be so callous as to dance on a battlefield among the bodies of the dead? What makes him want to dance amid death and devastation? Siva dances because he knows that death is always followed by birth, and destruction by renewal. He dances because the souls of the dead are passing on to rebirth and when an old order is swept violently away, it will be replaced by a new one, and hopefully a better one.

Siva dances in his fiery ring both at the end and the beginning of life, because one leads inevitably into the other. This is the Law of the Cosmos. Siva's "Cosmic Dance" is done at the beginning and the end of the Universe itself, because even Universes have no beginning and no end – only cycles. Before the "Big Bang" there had to be the death of the previous Universe, and after the death of our Universe there will be another "Big Bang", and a new Universe will be born.

If you think about these things you will find cause for optimism in any situation. When somebody dies, at that exact moment a baby is being born

– somewhere. While some mourn their dead, others are celebrating a birth. Life is a turning wheel.

There are several ways you can get out of negative thinking. First of all establish a dialogue with yourself. Talk to yourself as if to another person. Use a mirror if you like and really lecture yourself. Take hold of some of your favourite negative phrases and argue them out. Let us say, for example, that you believe you are ugly and unattractive. Look at your self in the mirror and you'll hear that old familiar negative you saying "God, what an ugly bastard I am. Look at me. Who could ever love ME!? UGLY!" Then ask yourself, "So what are you going to do about it? Wear a mask? Crawl into a hole in the ground and never come out? Hire yourself out as a scarecrow?" Be really sarcastic with yourself. And exaggerate! Say, "Hell, I'm so ugly it is a wonder the mirror hasn't cracked. Just look at that HORRIBLE face! I hate myself. I LOATHE myself. I am going to wear a mask, that's what I'll do. Be like the !!*!**! Lone Ranger. Or I will get myself a bell to ring so I can warn people to get their children indoors so they won't be frightened by this grotesque face of mine. Or maybe I'll just hide under the bed for the rest of my life!"

Do you see what is happening? You are beginning to see how ridiculous you are being. You may even make yourself laugh! And once you can laugh at your problems, you are half way home.

Now that you have talked yourself out of this negativity look in the mirror once more, but this time, say to yourself, "Okay, I am no film star, but I'm not THAT bad. I have seen uglier people than me. Do THEY get as depressed as I am? Hell no . . . look at Rod Stewart. All that money, all those beautiful girlfriends! What does HE think when he looks in the mirror first thing in the morning? Even I'm not THAT ugly! And what about that really GROSS woman down the street? Does SHE hide under the bed all day?

"Maybe I could do something about my hair . . . perhaps I could dye it; perhaps I could get it cut in a more flattering style. And as for my face – maybe if I looked after my skin a bit better and lost some weight I would be fine."

If you are a man, consider how you would look with a beard and/or moustache (or if you already have one, how you would look without it.) If you are a woman you can cover a multitude of sins with make up. If you really have a physical problem like an enormous nose for instance, make up your mind to stop complaining about it and see if you can get a "nose job" on the NHS.

Let's take another negative thought and give it the same treatment.

How about our old favourite, "I'm worthless. Useless. A burden on everyone. I am no good for anything and it would be better if I was dead." Okay, so what are you going to do about yourself?

If you are so absolutely worthless why are you still around? Why didn't you kill yourself long ago? Why don't you crawl into your grave right now and put a big sign up instead of a headstone, "Here Lies The Biggest Failure The World Has Ever Seen". But wait a minute – you don't even deserve a GRAVE, do you? They should grind you up and use you as fertiliser. But you would be no use even as fertilizer would you? What do you do with someone who cannot even make good fertiliser?"

After continuing this line of thought for a while you will begin to see how stupid it is. Hopefully you will see some humour in it too. Now you can sit back and start hacking away at this little chunk of negativity until there is nothing left. Get a pencil and paper and write down all your virtues as other people would see them. Come on now – there must be something. Are you intelligent? Maybe you are a bastard, but you're an intelligent bastard. Are you kind-hearted? A good parent? Do you sing? Can you dance? Do you write? Paint? Everyone has something they can do well. Perhaps your virtues are more physical. Perhaps you have a great figure, or nice legs. Maybe you have lovely eyes. Perhaps you are very strong. If you get stuck, ask a caring relative to help you. They will point out things you may not have been aware of.

If you have ever achieved anything in your life, note this down as well. 'O' levels, swimming certificates, sports trophies, war medals, university degrees – anything at all. Are you married? Do you have children? That is no mean feat you know – some people don't even have that. When you have completed your list, look at it and say to yourself, "Why should I feel I am worthless? This says I'm not worthless. I am no better and no worse than anybody else. Even if I were to die tomorrow I have made my little mark on the world – my bid for immortality! I have done this . . . and this . . . and these achievements are mine and mine alone. As each day passes I am slowly chipping out my name on the monument of time, so that I can live forever. I have done more than that old so and so down the road, that's for sure. What legacy have I to give to the world? My genes will live on through my children and my grandchildren . . ."

If you are childless like me you can still leave a legacy – you can still immortalise yourself. Poems, paintings, writing, or a beautiful garden you have created. All these will survive you. If you find you really do not have any achievements on your list and have never done anything of any worth, now is the time to start. Do something, anything, that will leave your mark on the world. Is there something you have always dreamed of doing but never had the time for? DO IT NOW! Look around you. What can you do to raise yourself just that little bit above your fellow men? Can you make or create something that will last?

One of the nicest ways to achieve immortality, and the easiest, is to plant a long-lived tree. Not any old tree, but a magnificent oak, or a chestnut; a beech,or a mulberry. Something that will live for a century or more. Imagine somebody sitting under your tree in four hundred years time, wondering who planted it.

You don't even need to buy a sapling – you can grow a chestnut or an oak from seed. As few people have a garden big enough for such a tree, find out if there is anywhere round about you could plant your tree. Most places have Countryside Groups who go out planting trees. There is nothing to stop you donating one in your name.

This year I have decided to grow a Bristlecone Pine. The Bristlecone Pine is the longest living tree on Earth. It can survive four THOUSAND years! How's that for immortality?

If you have a garden, get out there and turn it into the most beautiful garden in your street. Make it a garden people will admire. Watch them craning their heads over the fence in drooling envy. There is nothing stopping you but yourself.

If you can whittle wood, why not create some beautiful carvings? Make something that will become a family heirloom. My grandfather carved a chess set. He is dead now, but there will always be something of him in those beautiful little chess pieces.

Can you sew or embroider? Create something that will last like a tablecloth or quilt. Do you like photography? Aim to become an expert photographer and get your pictures published in the glossy magazines!

I could go on and on . . .

Goethe said:

"Lose this day loitering – 'twill be the same story,
Tomorrow – the next day more dilatory;
Then indecision brings its own delays
And days are lost lamenting over days,
Are you in earnest? Seize this very minute
What can you do, or dream you can, begin it!
Courage has genius, power, and magic in it,
Only engage, then the mind grows heated,
Begin it and the work will be completed!"

I keep this beside my desk all the time as a constant source of inspiration. Idleness is a state of mind, and is born out of negative thought. The Buddha said:

"Too cold! too hot! too late! such is the cry,
And so for those whose work remains undone
The opportunities for good pass by."

Finally, even the Bible says, "Go to the ant, thou sluggard; consider her ways, and be wise:" (Proverbs, 6:6.)

There is no excuse for anyone to sit around doing nothing all day. Whatever your particular talent, use it and exploit it. Then, even if it is nothing more than a hobby, at least you can say you have given it your best shot!

Take each and every one of your negative thoughts and give it the treatment explained in the examples above. Root them out and destroy them, or they will try to destroy you.

We all have ups and downs, good days and bad days. On your best days – those rare times when you feel free from depression and life seems good, grab a notebook and make the heading: "Reasons To Be Happy". Now write down all your positive thoughts and feelings. Tell yourself how lucky you are to have what you have, how well off you are compared to other less fortunate individuals, how much you have to be thankful for, how stupid you are to worry about silly things that may never happen, how the pressures on you are only imaginary, etc. etc . . .

Write in any positive thoughts that occur to you. Then, next time you feel low, get out this notebook and read through the list . . . Here you are reasoning with yourself, blowing holes in every one of your negative thoughts and feelings. After a while, you will find that although the negative thoughts still occur, they are quickly followed with the positive response you have written down. Beat down the Black Beast every time it raises its ugly head.

As well as countering your negative thoughts with positive ones, you need to ask yourself some very searching questions, and give honest answers to these questions. This may seem a strange thing to say, but are you using your negativity as a shield? Is it a way of avoiding the harsh realities of life?

If somebody invites you out to dinner, do you invariably turn them down, making all kinds of excuses, even though you feel mean? In your heart you know the only excuse is that you "cannot be bothered" or you "don't feel like it." The thought of having to feign happiness and face the strain of being in company is too much for you. Face up to your fears. Be honest with yourself, and admit the real reasons behind some of your negative actions, and tackle these. Do you fear going out? Do you fear being in company and therefore "being on show"? What are you really afraid of?"

Your opinion of yourself has more effect on the way you face the world than you might imagine. In my own case I found, on self-analysis, that I "lost my nerve" when I let negative thoughts about my own abilities come into my head. Most nervous people fear speaking in public – I had to sing in public, and although I was among friends I found myself overwhelmed with terror at the thought of standing up in front of all these people and singing to them. Then I realised that my fear was caused by negative thoughts that crept into my head without me realising they were there. I caught myself thinking that I was going to make a fool of myself, that my voice was terrible, and that I would forget the words of the song. I had made up my mind I was going to be a failure before I even began. I talked myself out of this by telling myself it wasn't exactly the Albert Hall, and nobody cared very much if my voice wasn't perfect. I also resorted to fantasy!

Fantasy is a much underrated form of positive thinking, and it can work wonders. Children use fantasy freely – a child living in a horrible rat-infested tenement may fantasise that he is a king in a palace, or a rock star in a Californian mansion. Through using these fantasies life in the tenement becomes bearable. Adults, unfortunately, see fantasy as childish and even unhealthy. An adult in a rat-infested tenement will have no fantasy world to escape into and life will become intolerable. Sometimes people in such situations resort to drugs, because the drugs do what childhood fantasies used to do – they offer a means of escape. This is very sad, and fantasies are much healthier than drugs.

While fantasy must be kept in its place, and must not be allowed to take over one's life, it can be used to make that life happier and more fulfilling. Fantasy can also help you in situations where your nerves are getting the better of you.

In my singing debut for instance, I fantasised that I was a famous country singer. After the Grand ole Opry this was chickenfeed. I imagined I was singing to adoring fans who had travelled miles just to see me. Famous singing stars do not worry about making fools of themselves or forgetting words, so I felt confident and carefree as I stepped in front of my audience. Nobody was aware of my fantasy, but it helped me through that evening.

There are many ways you can use fantasy to enrich your life and banish the blues. If you have to live in dreadful conditions you can make it more bearable by using fantasy. Imagine yourself as the hero or heroine of a novel undergoing a terrible ordeal. Imagine yourself brave and courageous in your sufferings, a martyr to your cause. Or perhaps you can imagine you are somebody completely different, living in another country. Since nobody can see into your mind, you can be whoever you choose to be, so long as it is in your fantasy. Fantasy can buffer you from the cruellest blows in life, bring sunshine into a grey world, and banish loneliness.

Remember how you used fantasy when you were a child? As you rode your bike down the street your weren't just John Smith riding a bike, you were Captain Smith the airline pilot, pointing your 747 down the runway. Or you were a policeman in a police car, rushing down the street with lights flashing and siren sounding! These little fantasies made the simple pleasure of riding a bike much more enjoyable, and you came home breathless and happy. Within reason, such fantasies can be used now, especially if you have to live in unpleasant surroundings, or do a boring, menial job.

When you have to dig the garden and it all seems like a lot of hard work for nothing, imagine you are the head gardener in a Victorian walled kitchen garden, and you are growing vegetables and flowers for the "Big House". If you have to live alone, and the walls are closing in, imagine you are a wealthy and successful film star relaxing in your Californian mansion. If you cannot sleep at night, imagine you are in a berth on board a ship, or travelling on a train, or any other place where you know you sleep like a log. Fill your day with little fantasies like this and cheer yourself up.

Your home can be made to echo your fantasies if you like. If you are always fantasising about being on a tropical island, fill your house with tropical plants, beach pebbles, driftwood, shells, and pictures of tropical beaches. If you like to escape into the past and love to fantasise about being in a past age, fill your home with the things of that time. If it is a particular country you fantasise about, fill your home with the things of that country.

Always remember that fantasy is the highest form of positive thinking, and dreams can come true. People who have always dreamed of winning the pools have won them, and everyone who emigrates to another country and a new life must have spent years dreaming about it. So do not belittle your fantasies. Use them constructively to improve the quality of your life. And always live with the quiet hope that one day your dreams may come true, because they might.

Depression and anxiety both result in a general feeling of weariness. Nervous exhaustion is caused by many things, including vitamin deficiencies, anaemia, and simple lack of life force – prana. Relatives and friends should understand just how "nerves" can sap a person's strength and make them feel totally exhausted. Many seriously depressed people give up the struggle altogether and take to their beds, too tired to cope. One reason for this is that only when you are in bed do people believe you are genuinely ill and leave you alone. If you are up and about the family expects you to carry on as normal, and society expects you to go out to work. What you desperately need and want is a sanctuary – some peaceful retreat where nobody makes demands on you and you can rest and recover. Peace – is this what you long for?

One of the "fatal" attractions of suicide is that death is looked upon as a sanctuary. Somewhere you will at last be able to rest in peace. This need for sanctuary must be understood by all who have to deal with the anxious, depressed, or mentally disturbed. They need to be given space and relieved of their duties for a while.

The brain is about as complex as the air traffic control system of a major airport, and like an airport control tower is must concentrate on many different functions at once. Try to imagine the brain as an air traffic control centre during the busiest time of the year. There are planes stacked up one above the other all waiting to land, more planes requesting permission to take off, and each has to be guided in or out of the airport without crossing the path of another plane and risking a collision. (Apparently the air traffic control systems at many major airports are overloaded; accidents waiting to happen.) Our brains, struggling to cope with 101 different tasks all at once are in somewhat the same situation.

In the mentally sick the system has broken down. Suppose during peak hours there was a crisis aboard a jumbo jet approaching the airport and it had to land immediately. All other traffic would be told to wait while the emergency was dealt with. Routine landings and takeoff's would cease, runways would be cleared, incoming planes diverted. All attention would be on the plane in trouble.

The sick brain is undergoing a crisis. It is fighting for survival. All attention is focussed on the illness that is causing the system to break down. Yet, in the midst of this crisis, sufferers are expected to concentrate on trivial everyday affairs. It is something like asking those overworked air traffic controllers to forget the jumbo jet about to crash and turn their attention to a little private plane on non-urgent business!

Relatives may even get irritable and abusive if the sufferer cannot "pull his weight" around the house, and employers often show a complete lack of understanding and sympathy. The illness must be acknowledged and sufferers must be given the peace and rest necessary to recover.

Having said this, the answer is not that sufferers should take to their beds and stay there. Given the opportunity, many depressed people do take to their beds, but this is done as a negative action and it merely makes the depression worse. So what do you do when you cannot cope any more and you desperately want rest?

The solution is to come to a compromise between one's own needs and the demands of the world around you. You will rest in bed and enjoy a little sanctuary, but you are not going to give up altogether. How is this to be accomplished?

We will take it that you have stopped working. Nobody should be expected to cope with the demands of a job as well as nervous illness unless the illness is particularly mild or the job is undemanding. If you just give in and take to your bed you are going to feel completely useless and perhaps guilty about your inability to cope. This will only add to your depression! What you must do is divide your day into periods of rest and periods of activity. Rest in bed is vital as it allows the body to heal itself, so don't feel guilty about your need for bed rest. But activity is also necessary.

When you decide to take your bed rest is up to you, but establish a routine of rest and activity and then stick to it. The best time for a rest is after lunch, or perhaps later in the afternoon. During your rest periods you can fully relax, free from all guilt, because you are not going to be completely useless. As soon as the rest period is over you will get up and return to your normal activities, refreshed and with renewed energy. Set small tasks for yourself every day – making lists if necessary, and then you can rest easy knowing you've done something useful that day. During your chores you won't feel so tired as you will have rested beforehand, and you know you can lie down against afterwards.

How much rest you take depends entirely on you and on how ill you are, but even if it lasts only fifteen minutes you should allow yourself a period of complete bed rest at least once a day. During this rest do not allow yourself to dwell on your problems. This is a good time to listen to soothing music, or read a good book. There is no need to sleep, just rest.

One good thing you must certainly do during rest periods is Positive Visualisation. Whatever it is you fear, you do not have to wait helplessly for the hand of fate to decide your destiny. You can influence your own karma by the power of the will. This technique does work, but you can only prove it to yourself by trial and error. Give it a fair chance though, and

BELIEVE in it. Tell yourself you are keeping an open mind and just for the present you are going to believe in it, because there is no point in attempting Positive Visualisation unless you do.

When you are fully relaxed and sleepy, conjure up a daydream about your problems being successfully resolved. Say you have an intolerable housing problem and you desperately want a move to a better house. Okay, so where would you like to live? Is there a house or street near you where you long to be? See yourself moving into the house of your dreams and visualise everything in as much detail as possible. And see yourself happy. Believe that this house is coming to you sooner or later. If you are offered a house that is not like your dream house refuse it, knowing that the house you want is coming. The next house you are offered could be it! Be single-minded. Don't accept what is not "right" for you.

You can use this technique to will up a job or a baby or anything else you want. Action is necessary as well of course. If you want a job you will need to apply for jobs, and if you want a baby, well – that requires action too.

If you visualise bad things happening to you all the time, you are unconsciously invoking them, and then you are surprised when these bad things actually happen! Visualise good things happening and bring good into your life. Thoughts are very powerful so don't will bad luck on yourself. Books on positive thinking will tell you to visualise yourself winning the pools or whatever, but if you really cannot see yourself winning the pools, and therefore cannot believe it is possible, you might as well forget it. Only visualise what is realistically possible for you.

Let your mind wander from one lovely daydream to another as you rest and never allow yourself to fret. Worry achieves nothing and only makes you ill. Look at your pets. There are plenty of things they could worry about but they don't. They don't give a damn about the future. When you were a young child did you worry about everything? Did you worry about what would happen if your parents were killed, or all the illnesses you could get? Did you worry about your father losing his job? Of course not. You sailed through life with never a care, in blissful ignorance of what might happen to you. That is why we all look back at our childhoods with nostalgia and say, "We never had any worries then." It is not that there WERE no worries, it is just that we didn't worry. Think about this for a moment.

Worry seems to be a defensive mechanism whereby the mind considers all possible troubles that could pose a threat to the well-being of the organism. You worry because you do not want to be caught "unprepared". It seems somehow unnatural not to worry, yet you will see that since worry achieves very little it is doing you more harm than good. The only way to stop worrying altogether is to learn absolute acceptance. Whatever it is you fear, tell yourself you will just have to accept it. Que sera sera – whatever will be, will be! Faith plays its part here. Have faith that whatever happens Higher Powers are watching over you, and someone up there does care. Every time you cross a road, drive a car, or step on board a plane, you are following your own individual karma and there is nothing you can do about it. If you are meant to die you will die. You cannot cheat death – unless of course you are not meant to die.

The singer John Denver dreamed of flying on board the Space Shuttle and he was overjoyed when he secured a place on the "Challenger". At the eleventh hour, however, he was turned down, and the teacher Christa McAuliffe was taken in his place. John was devastated. He had dreamed of this chance and it had been a dream come true. How could fate be so cruel? But as we all know, he was the lucky one. Christa McAuliffe, his replacement, died in the Challenger shuttle disaster. The Lords of Karma had ensured that John was not on that shuttle because it was not his time to die. I heard of one man who travelled on the train into London every day, but on the day of the Clapham Junction rail disaster he had been delayed and had missed the ill-fated train. That delay was no stroke of luck. It was meant.

We must learn to accept the fact of death. Everyone has to die, and in the course of many lifetimes we will all experience many different ways of dying, sometimes from accident, sometimes from disease; sometimes when we are young and sometimes when we are old. It is all grist to the mill. You must accept your fate, whatever it is, but the plus side is that acceptance frees you from fear. With acceptance comes serenity – a peace that cannot be shaken. Surrender yourself to your karma and stop fighting it. Trust God to guide you out of trouble.

We have dealt with your negativity and tackled your fears, but perhaps, instead of worrying about the future, its the past that haunts you? Perhaps your depression stems from an incident in your past?

Many people become depressed or mentally disturbed as a result of something that happened to them in the past, and eventually the original cause may be lost in the mists of time, leaving the depression lingering on under its own momentum. Can you trace your illness back to a single event or series of events in your past? Excorcise the ghosts of the past right now, and banish them from your life. You cannot go back and change the past but you may be able to do something to compensate for a negative past. Ask yourself, "What have I learnt from this experience?" and "How can I use this to help others?" Much good can come out of seemingly bad things.

Look at one of the worst things ever to happen to people in the modern world – the Holocaust. What this should have taught us is the evil of racism and anti-semitism, and how people can be brainwashed and led astray by the influence of one man. Unfortunately we do not seem to have learnt our lesson. Look at South Africa – are we seeing the beginnings of another holocaust there with black people as the victims this time?

Holocaust survivors should do all they can to spread this message, that we must live in peace with each other and take pleasure in our differences, rather than using them to fuel prejudice and hatred. Whatever you have suffered, try to turn it to good somehow. It may be hard to see any good in a terrible event when you are in the thick of it, but that good will come to light eventually.

"What seems at first a cup of sorrow is found in the end immortal wine" says the Bhagavad Gita (18:37).

Never allow any past event to "haunt" you. Talk to somebody, seek help, get your problems out into the open. Nowadays there are groups and organisations to help people with just about any problem you can think of. You are never alone. Whatever your problem is there are others facing the same problem. Find them and join them.

To sum up – you get back exactly what you send out. This is the Law of Karma. If you send out nothing but negativity, this is all you will receive. Positive thinking and positive daydreaming are vital to counteract this negativity. Drag out and exorcise the ghosts of the past, and accept your future, whatever it may be. Get yourself some good books on positive thinking and read all you can on the subject, never allowing yourself to become discouraged and sink back into old ways. Keep climbing up that ladder towards the light, and do not let yourself slip back, ever!

CHAPTER EIGHT

CONTACT WITH NATURE

"PET THERAPY" IS NOW WELL KNOWN, and many hospitals, old folks homes, and prisons have started Pet Programmes with remarkable results. Introducing animals into the lives of people who are withdrawn, sick or miserable, can work miracles. Autistic children are brought out of themselves by the presence of a furry, four-footed friend, and people who are alone and unloved find friendship at last.

One autistic child had never spoken a word and nothing anybody could do would bring her out of herself. She would sit as if in a trance, quite oblivious to the humans around her. Then one day her sterile institutional world was invaded by animals – dogs, cats, rabbits; even a donkey. They had been brought by an organisation who takes animals to visit people in hospitals and homes. When this lonely, silent little girl was introduced to a friendly dog it was as if a spell had been broken. She reached out, hugged the dog, and spoke her first word – the dogs name. Animals can get through to people where humans fail.

There was a prison in the United Stated where riots were an every-day occurence, and inmates and wardens feared each other in the pressure-cooker atmosphere of violence that pervaded the prison. Then a Pet Programme was introduced and in came the animals. The effects on previously violent prisoners was miraculous. Vicious murderers would handle pet canaries with a love and tenderness they had never shown to any human being.

The animals quickly became the centre of the prisoners lives, and they were fiercely protective of their charges. No animal was ever harmed, yet all these men were dangerous criminals. For some of the men it was the first time they had ever been loved or been able to give love. Now Pet Programmes are being started everywhere and animals are being brought into institutions all over the world, because the beneficial effect of animals on humans has been proven.

When people are placed in an institution they are isolated from nature. They no longer have contact with growing things or with animals. Only when people are removed from nature does it become obvious that contact with nature is essential for the health and sanity of mankind. In the words of a song, "You don't know what you've got 'till it's gone."

We have evolved as part of nature and are supposed to live in close contact with other life forms. In many institutions this ancient bond with nature is ignored and people are shut away in sterile, white-tiled hells where they never see a flower, or hear the birds singing, or bask in the sun, or caress the soft coat of an animal. Soon they get a blank look on their faces that shows they are well on the way to becoming human "vegetables".

We have all seen them when we have visited hospitals, haven't we? The frail jaundiced looking men and women sitting all alone in a corner, staring into space. They have given up on life and become living corpses. In the old days, people used to fear going into hospital in case they caught the dreaded "Hospital Disease" – a lethal infection. Now we have a new Hospital Disease!

What, I wonder, would be the effect if one of these human vegetables was taken out into a sundrenched green pasture, and set down among a sea of daisies and buttercups with one companion – a dog? I think we could guess. These "vegetables" would start to come back to life! They would laugh again, cry again, smile again. They might even get out of their wheelchairs and walk. It would be a wonderful sight, wouldn't it? Nothing has a more positive effect on the mood than fresh air, blue skies, sunlight, and young animals.

People who live and work on the land are nearly always healthier and happier than people who have to live and work in a concrete jungle. (Although sadly this is no longer as true as it once was. Farming is now becoming quite a stressful occupation.)

Mother Earth is a great healer and we should never underestimate her powers. A holiday in the country can do more good than years of doctors' prescriptions. Contact with plants and animals puts us in our place and shows us who we really are – part of nature, not above it. The animals are our brothers and sisters, and the earth is our true mother.

The smell of damp earth in the April rain, the scent of a rose, the smell of new-mown hay, the feel of a cool grassy lawn under one's bare feet, or the smell of the sea. There is hardly a human being alive who doesn't enjoy these things. Who isn't awed by the sight of a field of daffodils, or a woodland glade filled with bluebells? Or the maple trees turned red and gold in the Autumn.

The astronauts were so moved by the beauty of the Earth as seen from space that many have described it as a religious experience. They were also humbled to find that the Great Wall of China was the only visible man-made object. The beauty of nature exceeds all the works of man.

There is, at present, a great revival of paganism. The reason is that people have become sickened by the materialism of the modern world, and are reacting against it. The Judeo-Christian tradition appears to show little concern for the environment and even less for the welfare of other animals, and this causes some people to reject it and turn instead to a religion that is much more closely connected with nature. Churches are too often bleak and uninviting places, surrounded by litter-strewn, flowerless graveyards and dark, funereal yews. Pagan altars are decorated with flowers and many of the rites take place out of doors. The emptying churches and the drift towards paganism is just one symptom of the innate need for unity with the rest of the natural world.

Let Mother Earth heal you. Let her bind you in her gentle spell and make you whole again. And the best way to do this is to create a garden. No matter how small your plot is, start right now and turn it into a beautiful garden. "Oh I can't be bothered," I hear you complaining, "I'm too tired to do all that weeding and digging."

Believe me when I say your weariness will vanish once you get started. It might be a daunting prospect turning a weed-ridden yard into a garden, but think of the challenge! I have almost a quarter of an acre, and it was nothing but a field when I first broke the sod. But the satisfaction of seeing your garden gradually taking shape is indescribable. Draw up a plan first, so that you know exactly what you are aiming for, and start digging!

Anyone can be a gardener. It can cost as much or as little as you want it to, and your planned garden can be as simple or as time-consuming as you choose. If you do not know much about gardening, there are many books available on the subject. I would recommend the "Expert" series of books by Dr D.G. Hessayon (PBI publications), as these give the best value for money of any gardening books I have ever seen. "Armchair Gardening" with a good book is the best way to spend a wet afternoon or a cold winter's evening.

If you already have a garden, take another look at it. Is it a boring garden? Is there nothing more exciting than a few conifers? There are thousands of plants you could grow, so grow something interesting. And always set aside one part of your garden to grow vegetables in.

A garden is like a blank canvas. On it you can paint the picture of your choosing. It is an expression of your personality too, just like the clothes you wear. And just as dismal surroundings make you depressed, bright and cheerful surroundings will counter depression. Deliberately make your garden as bright and colourful as possible and it will aid your recovery. In choosing plants go for colour and scent. Just as colours can influence mood, certain plants have more positive "vibrations" than others, and you should make a point of growing these. Nasturtiums with their hot and almost luminous colours are a must. Marigolds – English and African, sweet peas, chamomile, Oriental poppies, honeysuckle, roses, and geraniums are other essential plants. Make your garden a "happy" one.

A garden can also be a sanctuary – a refuge from the outside world. Here you can relax in an atmosphere of peace and beauty and attune yourself to the rhythms of nature. Once you start gardening you will be well and truly "bitten by the bug" and you'll never regret it. It can be a lot more than a hobby. You can fill your kitchen with fresh fruit and vegetables, and produce armfuls of cut flowers – enough for every room in the house. Then if you are really keen, you can grow things to exhibit in local shows.

For most gardeners including myself, life would lose all meaning without a garden. The changing tapestry of colours and scents throughout the seasons is a perennial pleasure, and there is no healthier way of getting fresh air and exercise than by working in your garden. The best gift you can every give yourself is a beautiful garden and it will add a new dimension to your life.

Because the senses of a depressed person are blunted by the illness, your garden needs to be extra colourful, and filled with scent. Certain flowers appear to "radiate" happiness, and these should always be grown. Marigolds and mesembryanthemums are the best. For scent go for lilacs, roses, sweet peas, buddleias, lupins, heliotropium; and plants with fragrant foliage, such as lavender, mint, and the sweet briar or eglantine. A pond is almost an essential for the pleasure it gives you. It gives a cool and tranquil feel to the garden and will be a home for many different kinds of pond creatures, from water beetles to frogs.

If you do not have a garden, perhaps you have a balcony where you could grow plants in containers. Or if all else fails you can have windowboxes and hanging baskets. Fill these with scarlet geraniums and heliotropium (Cherry Pie) and they will give you a lot of pleasure. Consider getting the use of an allotment where you can grow vegetables and flowers, or offer to look after somebody else's garden in return for produce. If there really is no way you can have a garden, then you must create an indoor garden with house plants. I have over sixty, but you might not want to collect that many. Foliage plants are essential but do not rely only on these. Have flowering plants such as geraniums too, and bulbs in the spring. And remember that you can grow tomatoes and dwarf cucumbers on a windowsill. It really is amazing what you can grow indoors if you use your imagination. You can even grow orange and lemon trees from pips! These may never produce fruit, but make lovely foliage plants, and the leaves smell wonderful when handled. Essential indoor plants for victims of depression are scented-leaved geraniums, which can smell of roses, lemons, peppermint, and even coconut. Myrtle is another good windowsill plant that can be grown from seed and has fragrant foliage and flowers.

I have already described the many benefits to be obtained from contact with animals, and if you do not already have a pet, you are strongly advised to get one, even if it is nothing more than a cage bird or a goldfish. Cats are probably the best pet for nervous and anxious people, as they have a calming influence, but dogs might be better for depressed people as they have a stimulating influence, and dogs have to be walked, which forces you to get out into the fresh air.

Animals can give you an immense amount of love and companion-ship, and will prove to be better friends than any human being could ever be, remaining loyal to their dying day.

It is now known that stroking a pet slows down the heartrate and lowers blood pressure, so people with animals live longer. Lonely people also find that the presence of a pet comforts them. You can confide in a pet and share your deepest fears with them, and they will never mock you or betray you. Most of all an animal is something to talk to, so that there is no longer silence in the house.

The giving and receiving of love is essential to our well-being, and too many people are deprived of love. With animals in the house there is the opportunity to love and be loved, and their dependence on you gives you a reason to live, and a reason to get up in the morning. They NEED you, and it is a lovely feeling to be needed. Kittens and puppies will, moreover, amuse you for hours with their play and make you laugh, and I don't need to tell you that laughter is good for you. Pets, especially dogs, give you the perfect excuse to chat to people you meet, so that you can make friends.

If you lose a pet, you must look around for another one as soon as possible. It must be accepted that you will lose them, because their lives are shorter than ours, but once you get a new pet you soon find you are falling in love with it, and it will be as much of a companion as the old one. The surest cure for the grief that follows the loss of a pet, is the introduction of a new puppy or kitten and a fresh start.

CHAPTER NINE

MEDITATION AND MUSIC

MEDITATION IS NOT just for "hippies". All kinds of people are doing it now, and it is incredibly healing. Anxious people will find it of immense benefit in helping them to relax. Quite simply, meditation is a means of resting the mind. You can rest your body by lying down, but the mind remains active. Meditation stops all this mental activity and allows the brain some peace and quiet. It calms you down, stills your thoughts, and allows you to see everything in perspective.

Anybody can meditate, and you should set aside a period of about thirty minutes every day for meditation. There are various techniques including the well known "TM" – Transcendental Meditation, but TM relies heavily on mantras and the method I give you here is simpler; no mantras and no Indian gurus required.

Kneel before your little shrine or in front of a low table. On the table place a candle, which you will keep only for meditation. You can light a stick of incense too if you like as this creates a tranquil atmosphere. (Perfumes of all kinds are vital, and you should fill your home with beautiful scents. Perfume stimulates the senses and lifts the spirit. When the astronauts were deprived of perfumes in space they took to sniffing soap bars. Always wear perfume or aftershave and make full use of natural perfumes in your home. Scented plants and flowers, pot-pourri, scented candles, aromatic oils, and incense are better than artificial air fresheners.)

Having lit your candle and incense, make yourself comfortable and stare into the candle-flame. Keep your back straight (resting against something if necessary) and rest your hands on your knees or cup them one above the other in your lap. Now close your eyes and look into the darkness at a spot just in front of your nose. You should see a persistent image of the candle-flame there, gradually changing colour. Watch this until it fades, then imagine it is there. Alternatively you can use your imagination from the start, visualising as your focal point a lotus blossom, a rose, or the disc of the sun. The important thing is to look INTO the darkness, not AT it, as if searching for the fading image of the candle.

As you stare deep into the darkness, listen to the silence within you. Listen as if you were trying to hear a very faint sound, or a quiet whisper. Once you have achieved total concentration on silence and darkness, allow your mind to rest, letting go of all thoughts. Allow no thoughts to intrude on your inner peace, and if they do, lead your mind back to the silence. Aim for a state of complete serenity, where nothing can disturb you, and your whole being is at peace. Listen to your breathing and keep it slow and deep. Retreat within your own body as if you were a turtle, shutting out the world around you.

If you find it too difficult to concentrate on silence and darkness, even after some practice, you may need to try another technique. Visualise yourself in a beautiful city in some far away exotic place, walking down a tree-lined street. At the end of the street there is a square, and on the other side of the square there is a magnificent temple. This temple can be of any denomination you choose. It could be a church, a mosque, a synagogue, or a purely pagan temple. Slowly ascend the marble steps and pass through the door into the cool and peaceful interior. Here you will see yourself walking up to the altar where there are candles burning, and perhaps flowers, crystals, or anything else you would like. Kneeling before this altar you study the objects in front of you, let the tranquility of the place soak into you, and wait . . . Sooner or later someone may appear out of the darkness and approach you. Listen to what they have to say, and give them your problems and worries. This private temple is your own personal sanctuary, and you can visit it any time you want.

Once you have mastered meditation, you will find it highly addictive. The peace is wonderful and afterwards you will feel more rested than after a good nights sleep. Once you become a regular meditator, you will want to sit properly in the lotus posture, which is by far the best position to meditate in. Be warned however, for anyone unaccustomed to it, it is by no means easy, and you will need to have patience and keep trying.

Start by sitting on the floor with your ankles crossed, then, by slow degrees, pull in your feet towards your body until one heel is up against the perineum. Your knees should gradually sink down until one or both touches the floor. At this stage you can lift one foot and fold it over the other leg, tucking the foot into your groin. This is the half lotus. It will suffice for our purposes, and is really quite comfortable once the ligaments and muscles get used to it and the knee loosens up. There is no position that is so uncomfortable to begin with and so comfortable once you are accustomed to it.

If you have a pressing problem to solve, or a decision to make, you can meditate on it. Ask a question before you go into meditation, and keep it uppermost in your mind, but do not think about it. Just listen for the answer to come out of the silence.

You will find that your need for meditation grows and you will crave it whenever the clamour of the modern world gets too much for you. The best times to meditate are first thing in the morning, before lunch, or last thing at night. In a noisy environment use wax earplugs to shut out distracting sounds. These can be bought at any chemist and are recommended if you are bothered by noise and want thirty minutes or so of absolute peace. They are also useful if noise keeps you awake at night.

If you find yourself in a particularly stressful situation, such as a dentist's waiting room, or awaiting a job interview, or simply going through a "panic attack" you can use the technique I call the "Emergency Cut-Out", because it is a way of "switching off" your brain almost instantaneously.

What you do is to imagine you have zipped back in time and become a baby again. Now because you are a baby you have no knowledge of language and no experience of the world, so thinking is impossible. All you are aware of is the world around you as perceived by your senses. Your thinking processes have been frozen, and now you look around as if seeing the world for the first time. Allow your eyes to widen and relax, and scan the objects in the room with complete detachment. Look at everything, wondering at the shapes and forms you see, but passing on to the next object without any thoughts entering your head. Just look, but do not think about what you see. Once you master this technique you will be rewarded by a profound peace and freedom from all worry, and you can use this Emergency Cut-Out whenever and wherever you want. Still the turmoil within your brain and find a peace that you have never known before.

Music is a very powerful mood-altering force, and people underestimate just how much music can affect the emotional state. One particular song called "Gloomy Sunday" is notorious for the number of suicides it has caused. Now if music can drive you to commit suicide, then music is very powerful, and it follows that we can also use music to elevate the mood and make us feel happy.

With this in mind, choose your music carefully. Because it is so powerful, the wrong kind of music could deepen your depression and even lead to suicide! We are all tempted to play music that "suits our mood" when we are feeling unhappy. After a broken love affair, I remember playing the song "Without You" over and over again. There is a certain masochistic pleasure in forcing yourself to wallow in your misery by playing sad songs like this. This is all right if you are emotionally stable and you only let the misery last for one day. But it could be very dangerous for a seriously depressed person to do this. When somebody you love dies, you may want to play their favourite music over and over again, or play a record you both enjoyed together.

There is no doubt that some music has "bad vibrations" and can create a mood of hopelessness and unhappiness in anybody who listens to it. When somebody is already very depressed, playing such music could be the final "push" towards suicide. Beethoven's 5th symphony is one of these. Mike Oldfields "Moonlight Shadow" is another. Both are beautiful pieces of music, but very dangerous for anyone who is deeply depressed. Other songs may be depressing because of their association with somebody or something that makes you sad.

Avoid at all costs any music that makes you feel miserable. Also avoid acid rock, punk rock, and the heavy type of classical music (such as Beethoven's 5th) so favoured by classical radio stations. Go for light, cheery, and uplifting music. So-called "New Age" music is now available, and is recommended. Note what feelings your favourite pieces of music produce in you and "ban" any that leave you feeling sad, angry, or irritable. On the other hand if a certain piece of music makes you feel joyful and uplifted, start playing this more often.

Begin a collection of "positive" music, right now. If you hear a piece of music you particularly like on television (even if it is just incidental music or background music) write to the television company and ask what it is, enclosing an SAE. The television companies are very helpful in this area and may even give you the record number so you can order it. The television is a good source of "positive" music if you keep your ears open for it.

Gradually build up a collection of tapes and records that are relaxing, uplifting, and inspiring. Some people have a radio going all the time, whether they are listening to it or not and regardless of what is being played. This is very bad as you are filling your head with unwanted noise and perhaps with the wrong type of music. Do not be afraid of silence. If you play a lot of positive music you will memorise the pieces and then you can "play" one of them in your head any time you want. Start being very choosy about the music you listen to, because music affects not just the conscious mind but the subconscious also. Be you own D.J. and only allow yourself to hear music that will cheer you up.

If you really want to exploit the power of music in beating your depression, concentrate on "Air" music and, to a lesser extent, "Water" music. Yes, music can be classified according to its ruling element, just like food. If you prefer, you are classifying it according to its "vibrations" which are suggestive of one or other of the elements. Air music "uplifts" you and has a soaring and expansive feeling to it, making you feel happy, optimistic, and fit. The famous "Chariots of Fire" theme tune is typical air music, and another is Verdi's "Chorus of the Hebrew Slaves" – which is just about the most positive piece of music there is. British Airways used it to great effect in one of their television adverts. Other pieces of "air" music are "Regata dei Dogi" by Rondo Veneziano, and all the South American pan pipes music. Water music is soothing and relaxing, like a tropical lagoon. Hawaiian music is typical, but so is Madonna's "La Isla Bonita". For obvious reasons the air music is better for depression sufferers, and water music is better for anxiety sufferers. If you think all this is nonsense, put it to the test. You will see for yourself how air music can make you feel much happier and more positive, and water music will relax you.

Music can be combined with meditation. Choose a favourite piece of music and conjure up happy daydreams to go with it. Lose yourself completely in the music and forget about the world around you. Mike Oldfields "QE2" for instance, is a combination of air and water and is very positive. You could imagine yourself on the deck of an ocean liner, enjoying the cool sea spray. The track "Arrival" is extremely positive and I use it for the "Light Visualisation" and "Jet Stream Visualisation" exercises.

Make use of music then. Fill your home and your head with beautiful, uplifting, and comforting music and never allow yourself to listen to any music that will fill you with negative feelings.

CHAPTER TEN

ACTIVE MENTAL EXERCISE

DEPRESSED PEOPLE TEND to withdraw from the world and become apathetic about life in general. Depression loves boredom, and far too many depressed people become "couch potatoes", watching television all day, over-eating, and perhaps worst of all – chain-smoking. To counteract this you must keep your mind active and stimulated at all times. Do not be a vegetable. It is all too easy to moan, "Oh I can't be bothered," but mental stimulation requires little or no effort.

Reading a good book is probably the best way to keep the mind active, and the sort of books you should read are the ones which broaden your horizons and expand your mind, increasing your knowledge of the world around you. Read travel books, books on natural history, science, hobby subjects, geology, "New Age" subjects and biology. Leave trashy fiction on the shelf – it won't do you any good.

Use your local library. Go to the library regularly and seek out interesting books that will teach you something new. Make lists of books you want to read and ask the library to order them for you. I know of no better place to "kill time" than in the library. It is warm, quiet, and there is plenty to read.

Learning is a powerful antidote to depression. Have you ever noticed how students seem to possess an enthusiasm for life that working adults have lost? Those halls of learning change people, bringing them out of themselves and allowing them to realise their full potential as human beings. A conversation with students is usually refreshing and stimulating, and the reason is partly that they can talk knowledgeably about a wide variety of subjects, and partly because of their sheer zest for life!

"Hot House Children" – children who naturally or by design are child geniuses – always have vibrant personalities. They positively "ooze" with enthusiasm for life and the world is their oyster. It has been proved by "Hot-housing" children from an early age that constant mental stimulation actually increases the intelligence. Lack of mental stimulation on the other hand, could reduce intelligence due to the loss of unused brain cells.

Do not be afraid of learning. It can do nothing but good. Study and learning ignites the brain and sweeps through it like a storm-driven fire. Depression doesn't stand a chance. Learning is no less than one of the chief purposes of life, so learn all you can. Be all you can be . . . reach for the stars . . . DO IT!! There is nothing more positive than learning, and there is so much you can learn. Do not stop studying the moment you leave school. The brain is like a muscle; if muscles are exercised properly they grow bigger and stronger, but when they are unused they wither away. Are you letting your brain waste away? Use that grey matter, and find out how much fun studying can be. Learn a new language, study one of the sciences; choose any subject that interests you and aim to become an expert at it.

While going to classes is undoubtedly the best way, there is nothing to stop you studying at home in your own way, using your library and perhaps specialist book shops, college book shops, and specialist libraries. This way you can study at your own pace and never have to worry about exams. Your specialist subject can be absolutely anything. Just look at the variety of subjects covered in "Mastermind"!

I have lost count of the times I will be talking about gardening for instance, (my specialist subject) and people will shake their heads and say, "Oh I don't know the first thing about that!" Well there is nothing to stop them learning, is there? Each time you come up against a subject you know nothing about, take a mental note of it, and aim to find out more about it.

Above all, learn all you can about the world you live in. Can you name all the birds that visit your garden? Can you name all the flowers you see, both wild and cultivated? How many stars can you name? How many constellations can you identify? Can you name the different types of clouds in the sky? Do you know anything about the anatomy of your own body?

Apart from stimulating the brain and increasing intelligence, knowledge does something else. It gives you a new pride in yourself. At last you will feel worthwhile. This is very important for depression sufferers.

What television programmes do you watch? If your television diet consists of nothing but soap operas, game shows, and sport, then shame on you. There are many excellent documentaries and scientific programmes on television that should not be missed, as well as breathtaking natural history films.

Many people complain that television watching is harmful, but it depends on what you watch. I wouldn't be without a television. On my income I could not afford to travel the world, yet I can explore the jungles of New Guinea, watch wildlife on African savannas, dive into the deepest reaches of the oceans, see the life on a coral reef, look inside a termite mound, see the Earth from space, watch a baby developing in the womb, and look at the strange, microscopic world revealed by an electron microscope. And all this without ever leaving my armchair! Television enables you to see what would normally be barred to you, and go to places you would never otherwise be able to go. But none of this is any good if you don't watch the right programmes.

There are specialist programmes on television for schools and colleges. Have you ever watched any of them? I think you would be pleasantly surprised, and you could learn quite a lot if you watched all of them. Education no longer has to be boring.

People who for one reason or another cannot get out, or people who are bedridden or disabled could do nothing better than to watch all the educational programmes, taking notes if necessary, and study a wide variety of subjects.

What do you read? Newspapers are best kept to a minimum or ignored altogether as they contain far too much misery. Newspapers merely serve to fuel your fears and deepen your depression, especially since the journalists always exaggerate everything. Some people seem to have a morbid fascination with newspapers. They have the paper delivered every day without fail and they immediately pour over the doom and disaster stories with relish. Then they turn to the "Deaths" column to see who has died!

When you talk to these people all you get from them is, "Isn't it terrible about that air crash!" and "Did you know so and so had died? You didn't? It was in the paper this morning. Tragic, so tragic!"

Do away with this kind of misery. It does you no good whatsoever and will only serve to intensify your depression. If papers depress you, why buy them? I never buy a paper. I watch the news on television once a day only. You soon hear about anything important, don't worry. It is better to spend your money on more cheerful and interesting reading matter such as weekly and monthly magazines.

Avoid books that dwell on the macabre, and the kind of science fiction that revolves around "nightmare worlds" and the destruction of all life on Earth. Choose books that have a happy ending. You do not want to fill your head with anything that could feed the Black Beast.

Discover the beauty of poetry; good, old-fashioned poetry, not this modern, disjointed stuff. Good poetry is music with words, and is at once a symphony of words and a picture painted in thought. Read the works of the old poets – Shelley, Keats, Longfellow, De La Mare, and Coleridge, and also poems that are primarily written for children but are too good just for kids.

My English teacher in primary school used to read from a wonderful book called "The Book of a Thousand Poems" (Evans). I loved it so much I went out and bought a copy for myself. This is a fine book for families.

Begin a collection of your favourite poems, either photocopying them, or copying them out by hand into an exercise book. One of my most treasured possessions is a hard cover exercise book titled "The Seasons". In it I have copied out five pages of poems for every month of the year, and I get a great deal of pleasure from reading it. I also paste pieces of cartridge paper with poems on them over the date panels on old calendars I want to keep for the sake of their pictures. This gives me a picture and two or three poems for each month of the year, together with a note of jobs to be done in the garden.

My "Seasons" book has some of my own poems in it, as well as poems by many different poets, old and new. Have you every tried writing poetry? It is an excellent way to express yourself and capture the atmosphere of special moments in your life. Marking the passage of the seasons in this way will make you take notice of what is going on in nature, and is another way of forcing your attention outwards, away from yourself.

Keeping a diary is an excellent way of analysing yourself, and you can soon learn to be your own psychiatrist. But the kind of pocket diary that only allows you one or two lines per day is useless. Use memo books or larger notebooks, and if necessary you can write up a whole page. Record all your feelings, both positive and negative, and read back over old entries every once in a while. You will probably find it quite an eye-opener. Faults in your attitude to life and your expectations of it are glaringly obvious, and you will be able to see just how negative you are. You can also use your diary to express emotions and fears you could never share with another human being.

A gardening or weather diary is another idea. Recording the weather can become a full-scale and very absorbing hobby if you invest in some basic meteorological recording equipment.

All these ideas are ways of turning your attention away from yourself, and this is essential if you have a lot of time on your hands. Try always to appreciate the little pleasures of life. Eat slowly and really enjoy the various flavours in your food. Savour the exotic taste of tropical fruits. Enjoy a spectacular sunset or a rainbow. Even such simple things as a good cup of tea, the sun sparkling on a crystal vase, and the smell of a new bar of soap can become real pleasures if you stop rushing around long enough to think about them and enjoy them fully. Don't go through life blinkered. Take your time and LOOK, LISTEN, FEEL! If you have time on your hands make the most of it to appreciate the little things working people have no time to even notice.

Unemployment poses its own special problems and is undoubtedly a chief cause of depression. From a busy nine to five routine you suddenly find yourself with more time on your hands than you know what to do with. It is a strange thing, but working people dream of being able to have unlimited free time, while, to the unemployed that free time becomes a nightmare. When you are working you think how wonderful it would be to be free and easy, with all the time you want to do exactly what you wish. You could lie in every morning, no more commuting, no more aching feet at the end of the day, no more stuffy offices. Unemployment ought to be welcomed with open arms, so why isn't it?

The truth is that after the novelty of unlimited free time has worn off you get bored, and then you just do not know how to fill all those hours. Retired or disabled people face the same crises. They may have made all kinds of plans, but when the time comes they find the days are just too long. You may have planned to go fishing and play golf, but these hobbies won't take up all your time, and what do you do when it rains? You may have planned to travel the world, but then you find you cannot get very far on an unemployment benefit. The sad fact is that too much free time leads to boredom, irritability, and depression.

Part of the problem is that without a job you feel "excluded" from the rest of humanity, and a feeling of worthlessness sets in. People are identified with their jobs, as if the job was somehow a part of them like colour of hair and zodiac sign. You only have to watch quiz programmes on television to see this. Contestants are invariably introduced as: "John Smith, 36, fork lift truck driver" and "Jane Smith, 29, secretary". This is really quite illogical when you think about it, and even unfair! John Smith may hate his job and may never see himself as a fork lift truck driver. Jane Smith may be a university graduate who cannot get a job and had to take whatever she could get until a more suitable position comes along. Only professional people have actually chosen their jobs – most people end up doing jobs they do not particularly like. But as long as people are identified with the jobs they do, people without jobs are going to be made to feel somehow inadequate as human beings.

This is silly really, as employment is an invention of modern man, just like the car and the vacuum cleaner. Animals do not work in the way we define work. "Yes but animals have to hunt or forage for their food," you may say. Since the object of the game is to put food on the table, why should an unemployed man labouring in his garden and supplying most of the family's food still be made to feel guilty about not working? He IS working. Try to see unemployment in its proper perspective. You are not less of a person because you do not have a job. So long as you occupy your time in a creative and constructive manner and can still put food on the table there is no reason to feel ashamed. Man invented work and it is the fault of man that there is unemployment in the first place. Don't blame yourself.

The shame attached to unemployment can lead people into what I call the "Self-Destruct Mode". They stop caring about how they look, stop caring about their future, and, in the end, stop caring about looking for work. They slouch around on street corners and indulge in "self-destructive" habits such as drinking, smoking, and drug-taking. This negative way of life can only lead you deeper into the mire, so that your lifestyle becomes even more self-destructive. The bottom line is imprisonment, a mental hospital, or death, depending on what direction your self-destruction takes!

The first thing to happen when you enter Self-Destruct Mode is that you lose interest in your appearance, or adopt an "alternative" appearance that tells the world what you are doing. If you hang about street corners in "distressed" denims and dye your hair green, you are saying you have opted out of society and are no longer in the market for a job – because it is very unlikely you would get a job looking like that!

The next stage is that you begin to adopt self-destructive habits. This is the very worst thing you can do, because not only will excessive alcohol, cigarettes and drugs undermine your health, but they will take what little money you have left. Recognise the signs of self-destruction and stop it before it leads you into complete ruin.

Getting a job demands that you first sell yourself at the all important interview, and it is a very competitive market. It is essential therefore to keep up appearances and resist all temptation to adopt self-destructive habits. Self-destruction is the result of negative thinking such as, "I don't care anymore", "Why should I bother?" and "To *!!* with everything!" and this negative thinking must be nipped in the bud.

So how can you handle unemployment positively? Well, think of it this way. Here is a wonderful opportunity to improve yourself and therefore your chances of getting a job. Get onto a training scheme if there is one, or go to adult education classes. Everybody could use a few more academic qualifications, so get those grades you didn't get when you were at school. Go back to school as a mature student if necessary, or study at home with the Open University. There are a vast number of home study courses available – anything from Sociology to Chiropractic and Herbalism. The big drawback with all of them is that they cost quite a bit of money, and will involve travel to sit exams etc. Because of this, it is sensible to enrol on these courses immediately you find yourself unemployed, while you still have some money in the bank. Such courses will not only occupy you and give you a real sense of worth, but they can lead to a new and rewarding career.

An alternative to study is to exploit some talent you have which has so far been ignored. Now is the time to write that book you have always wanted to write, or try your hand at painting or pottery. Or you may want to do something adventurous like trekking across India or going to the South Pole. You could volunteer to help some charity, either at home or abroad, and volunteers are always wanted for charity work in homes, hospitals, or local schemes.

Always keep yourself in good physical shape and keep mentally alert. Crafts can be found that will fill your time and put a few pennies in your pocket as well. Of all the hobbies you can do to fill your time, none is better than gardening. It can take up as much of your free time as you let it, and you can spend just what you can afford on it. It also satisfies the human male's natural urge to provide for his family, since you can grow most of your own food.

Disabled people are unable to get out and about much, but there is still plenty you can do to fill your time and keep the mind active. Hundreds of crafts will be suitable, and you can study "New Age" subjects such as crystals, aromatherapy, herbs, palmistry, astrology, the Tarot, – whatever takes your fancy. Writing to penpals is another very good way to pass the time.

Depressed and anxious people may well be more "sensitive" and more creative than others, and this can be put to good use. "Hot house" yourself and ferret out whatever talents you have. You will not only keep your mind active, but you may discover a whole new way of life!

CHAPTER ELEVEN

SPIRITUAL SUPPORT

LAST, BUT NOT LEAST, never forget the power of prayer. Whatever your faith, turn to God for comfort whenever you feel the need, and do not be cynical about religion. As I said earlier, people often lose their faith because they feel God has let them down. They cannot understand how a loving God can permit such tragedy and suffering in the world and they conclude that there is no God. I hope by now you will understand that God neither permits nor forbids tragedy and suffering – such things are due to karma, and they happen because they must. God may have set the wheels of karma in motion but he rarely, if ever, interferes with it, and allows it to follow its own course according to the natural laws which govern it. As a clock must strike the hour once its mechanism is set in motion, so we must face a crisis in our life when the time comes. God, of course, understands the reasons for tragedy and suffering, and we don't. He knows these things must happen, but that doesn't mean He doesn't care about us. In the hour of greatest need He is there, as anyone who has undergone an ordeal will tell you.

A child will never learn to walk if it is carried everywhere, and we must be allowed to flounder our way through our karmas until we find our feet and are able to stand up and hold our heads up high. Like a loving father God will encourage us in our efforts to overcome our difficulties, comfort us when we fall, and rejoice with us when we finally win through. This is so right and so sensible, yet people rage at God if He does not rush to their aid every time life gets a bit rough. Believe me when I say that God weeps with you when you are in trouble. He wants to give you His love and guidance and it must hurt Him deeply when you reject Him. Try to regain your faith, because nothing is more comforting in times of need. When all the world is against you, and you feel completely alone, you always have God. He is there when all others have deserted you.

Now, I am not advocating fanatical religious belief. Being fanatical about anything is unhealthy and can be dangerous. There are many who would lure the vulnerable into the more extreme forms of religious expression. But try to be quietly and privately pious and let your faith support you through troubled times.

There is no need even to go to a church or a temple if you don't want to. Keep your own little shrine within your house and pray there whenever you like. Endeavour always to have some fresh flowers on this shrine, candles, and perhaps an incense burner. Anything else will depend on your own personal beliefs, but things such as healing crystals, rosary beads, and sacred books are all suitable.

If you find it impossible to regain your original faith, perhaps you could explore other faiths and find a new path to God. Do not be afraid of doing this; adopting a new religion can give a whole new meaning to your life. Study all the chief religions of the world, for they all have something to teach, and they help you to see life from many different angles. Read all the sacred texts – The Bible, The Koran, The Bhagavad Gita, The Upanishads, The Talmud, Buddhist teachings, etc. Each one offers a different perspective of the same basic truths, and it gives you plenty of food for thought. There is more than one path to God and it is up to each of us to choose the path that suits us best. Don't let anyone tell you that any one religion is the "right" one while all others are "wrong". This is how persecution is born.

Nobody owns your soul, and you have a right to choose your own spiritual path. Many people have suffered terribly through religious persecution, and it is an evil that is still with us. It can happen on a large scale – such as the festering evil of anti-Semitism – or on a small scale, such as when one member of a family rejects the family faith and joins an obscure sect the family disapprove of. Everyone must find their own way through life and their own spiritual niche. The only "rights" and "wrongs" of religious belief are the necessity of following what is known as the "Right Hand Path" rather than the "Left Hand Path". All the main religions of the world are "Right Hand Path". The Left Hand Path is that of Satanism and black magic and for your own sake you should avoid this path at all costs! (WHITE magic, and WHITE witchcraft – Wicca, is on the Right Hand Path, not the Left. Do not confuse them. If anyone has been persecuted more than the Jews it is witches, and this persecution comes from pure ignorance).

A religion that instils fear and persecution in its followers is a bad religion. Karmic liability must be accepted for any action taken by a person that will alter another person's life. Missionaries may believe that they are "saving" people, but by coercing people to join faiths that are unsuited to them they are harming these people, not helping them.

Becoming a Jehovah's Witness or a "Born Again" Christian may have saved the missionary's soul, and had nothing but the most positive effect on his life, but the same thing may not be true for somebody else! Don't be inflenced by anybody else then, no matter how persuasive they are, and make up your own mind about which religious path you should follow. If you meditate on the matter, sooner or later the answers will come to you.

Remember that God will always love you, so long as you love Him, and He will forgive your sins providing you accept the karma they have incurred, and you truly repent. No matter how great your sins, if you go down on your knees right now and ask God to forgive you, telling Him you truly repent and you accept karmic retribution for your sins, whatever this may be, the VERY ACT OF REPENTANCE notches up some karmic credit for the future. You may be unable to avoid the karmic retribution that will surely come – in this life or the next – but with this your sufferings will end, so long as you continue to live the right way from now on.

Write a prayer down on paper – a letter to God, and read this every time you pray. Don't pray only for yourself – pray for others too, both humans and animals. If you make a promise to God you must keep it. And always remember to thank God for the blessings you have at the moment, even if they are just a roof over your head and food on your table. There is always somebody worse off than you are. Think of them when you feel life has treated you unfairly, and give thanks for what you have.

God does care about you and He is watching over you now. He wants you to find your own solution to your problems because that is how you learn and become spiritually mature, but He is always with you. Think about it – if God bailed you out every time life got a little rough for you, your very existence would be pointless. If you look back at all the bad things that have happened to you, and ask yourself, "What did I learn from this?" and "How has it changed me?" you may be surprised at the good that has come out of them! You may be able to see a link between a series of events. It is almost as it you were a pawn on a giant chessboard, something like Alice in "Through the Looking Glass", where there was an adventure in every square. God is thinking five moves ahead when he allows some tragedy to befall you. Without knowing what lies in wait for you five moves ahead you see the tragedy as pointless and cruel! So accept it with serenity and go with it, not against it, and one day, you, the humble pawn, will reach the eighth square and become a "queen"! Then you will be able to look back and say, "Well of course, that's why such and such happened. If it hadn't, then such and such would not have followed and I wouldn't be where I am now" Suddenly it all makes sense and everything comes together. You can pick out these hidden "Trails of Karma" in a lot of situations if you look for them. Sometimes it is really remarkable how an end result rests on a single twist of fate – a chance meeting or being in the right place at the right time. At times like these you get an insight into how karma works and you can unravel the knot of fate that weaves tortuously through your life.

Your illness is a negative reaction to the circumstances you find yourself in. It may be a karmic ordeal or merely a karmic hiccup, but whatever the cause of your illness, it is up to you to take control of your life and pull yourself out of it so that you can fulfil your purpose on this Earth. If you think about it you will realise that being negative about everything will not help you, and will only add to your pain.

The responsibility for the rest of your life is yours. You cannot escape this. Suicide is not the answer, since this will only mean you will have to face the same troubles again in the next life, and again, and again, until you learn to overcome them and learn their lesson. But surrendering to karma gives you peace, so stop fighting, accept your lot, and affirm that you are going to work towards a better life as from now.

The power to change is in your hands. Rise up with courage and determination, and take your Black Beast by the horns. Fight depression every step of the way, because this – this shadow within you, is your greatest enemy! If you want to be happy and you want a better life, you MUST overcome it.

"Arise therefore! And with the help of thy Spirit lift up thy soul: allow not thy soul to fall. For thy soul can be thy friend, and thy soul can be thine enemy." (Bhagavad Gita 6:5)

"Arise, shine; for thy light is come." (Isaiah 60:1)

Summary

YOU ARE YOUR OWN WORST ENEMY. It is not the world that is against you – YOU are against YOURSELF. It is important to realise that it is only your outlook on life that is at fault, and not the circumstances of that life. Be honest with yourself. Even if your circumstances changed, before long you would lapse into depression again. You would find fault in your new house, or your new partner, or your new way of life as much as the old. Your old worries would be replaced by new ones because you are a worrier.

I used to live in a town and hated it. I dreamed of moving to the country and was sure that if I could just get out of the town and have a home in the country I would never be depressed again. Well my dream came true – I was able to move to a farm. Was this the end of my depression? For a while, yes. But it wasn't long before I began to complain about my new home, and about life in the country. After a few years I was every bit as depressed as before and dreaming of the town!

When I moved into my present house I thought once again that I would leave my depression behind me, but just as before, it followed me to the new house. I realised then that wherever I went I would still suffer from depression and my circumstances had little to do with it. The fault was in me. Circumstances can improve or increase your depression but you will still be basically depressed.

Stop thinking of yourself as a victim of circumstances beyond your control, and realise that you have the power within your own hands to transform your life. Things may be very difficult for you, and you may be undergoing a crisis, but there are always people who are worse off than you are, so think of them and count the blessings you have. Accept your karma, whatever it is and don't try to swim against the current. See ordeals as challenges to be overcome. Resign yourself to whatever pain and suffering you must bear, because fighting it will only make it worse. If you find your suffering hard to accept, try looking at it as something you are doing for others – a sacrifice you are making to God. When in pain, physical or mental, say over and over again:

"I am the pain-bearer!
I take upon myself all their suffering!
I suffer that they might be freed from suffering.
The greater their pain, the greater my pain.
I am the pain-bearer!
Let ME bear the pain!"

While saying this prayer, visualise the humans or animals you wish to remove suffering from. Will that their pain shall be transferred to you so that they are freed from it. The surprising thing about this is that you will find your pain immediately lessens. It is almost as if some Higher Power takes mercy on you and rewards you for your selfless act of sacrifice. Christians have always made themselves martyrs by suffering for the sake of others, following the example of Jesus on the cross. But you don't have to be a Christian to make your suffering an act of sacrifice.

When I am in pain I think of all the animals who suffer because of the brutal inhumanity of mankind, and I am suffering for them, taking their pain upon myself. I have quite a bit of physical pain to bear and this helps. It gives my pain a purpose.

However depressed you are now, I can assure you I have been there too. I have been a hairsbreadth away from suicide several times in my life, so I know what it feels like. You can see no hope whatsoever for the future, and no reason to keep struggling on with a seemingly pointless existence. There is a feeling of unreality, as though you are dreaming and are not properly awake, and the world may assume the atmosphere of a nightmare. People become cardboard cut-outs – faceless, soulless creatures who do not seem to care if you live or die. And all beauty is eclipsed by sorrow and pain until it seems that all the world is against you. Life loses its meaning and there is a dark cloud hanging over you, blotting out the sun. Oh yes, I know only too well what it is like to be overwhelmed by depression!

Some people reach a crisis point where they attempt suicide, while others kill themselves slowly through abuse of drugs and alcohol. They have slipped into the "Self-Destruct Mode", and can't get out of it.

About six years ago I hit rock bottom after a long period of ever deepening depression. One thing seemed to pile on top of another until I was at breaking point. When my dog was run over by a car and had to be put down it was a case of "the straw that broke the camel's back". I just snapped! As I buried my dog I told her not to worry because I would be joining her very soon. On that dark November day I climbed the stairs for the last time, locked myself in my bedroom and loaded a shotgun. I felt I had nothing more to lose and nothing to live for. I wept because it had come to this, but I was resigned to death. It was only a strange supernatural intervention that stopped me blowing my brains out right there and then. Whether you believe the supernatural part of the story is not important. What is important is how it helped me to see things as I had never seen them before, and how I changed as a result.

I was sitting there, staring at the gun, when I suddenly became aware of a strange golden light on the wall in front of me. This was in the depths of the countryside and it was nearly dark, so there was no outside source of light. Indeed, it was the fact that this ball of light had no source which drew my attention to it. While I was puzzling over this I felt a "presence" in the room, near my left shoulder. It was indefinable but benevolent, and I just knew I was no longer alone.

The "presence" directed me to watch the circle of light on the wall, and in it I saw moving pictures – like pieces of a home video. I saw myself and incidents from my past life, and in each incident I was appalled at myself, for I was so full of hatred and resentment and bitterness, and seemed to be forever raving at something. The "presence" with me was trying to make a point, and suddenly it clicked and hit me like a bombshell. My attitude to life, had, for a very long time, been completely negative. It wasn't the world that was against me – it was ME who was against MYSELF. All this negativity I had been putting out was coming back to me under the Law of Karma, and this was the cause of my most recent troubles. I had caused my own downfall. I was responsible for my own suffering, and I was destroying myself.

I realised then that everything that had happened to me was my own fault – a result of my negativity – and that I now had the power to change it all. I could turn my life around and drive away the darkness that had engulfed me.

As soon as I had come to terms with this revelation "the presence" faded away, and I was all of a sudden filled with the most tremendous joy and enthusiasm. My life was in MY hands and I knew now what I had to do. I could choose to die in misery, or I could overcome my difficulties with positive action and go forward to a wonderful new life. I do not need to tell you which choice I made.

In a mere hour or so I was completely transformed and I have never looked back since.

Under Karmic Law we are all responsible for our own destinies, and we (unwittingly perhaps) create our own heaven or our own hell. Ask yourself – do you REALLY want to wallow in misery for the rest of your life? Do you REALLY want to carry on as you are now? Or do you want a better life? The choice is yours my friend. You can be happy again, and you can be fulfilled but you will have to work at it. Start right now and change your lifestyle and your attitudes to life, banishing all that is negative, and go forward to a new life with hope. It could take five years or more, but eventually you will be able to see the first rays of sunlight breaking through your darkness, and you will shout, as Pheidippides did on reaching Athens from Marathon, "JOY! WE WIN!" What a marvellous day that will be.

Death seems very attractive indeed when you are in the depths of depression, but remember, it will not offer you freedom from your problems, because the very purpose of your life is to solve those problems. You live so that you can learn and your sufferings are part of that learning. If you give in to melancholy and take the coward's way out you will have to face the same problems all over again in the next life. A horse that refuses a fence is taken round to face it a second time. You will be confronted with the same problems time and time again until you face up to them and work them through. Only then, when the lesson has been learnt, will you be rewarded with peace. Then it will be the peace of one who has fought a spiritual battle and returned a hero, or has been through a raging storm and can now lie down and sleep in the sun.

Each of us has a cross to bear. I have mine and you will have yours. Nobody escapes the trials and ordeals that life is all about, although it may sometimes appear that there are individuals who are particularly favoured by destiny. But you do not know what personal agonies these "lucky" people are going through, or what may befall them in the future. "The devil always takes his dues" and luck can turn sour. Never get too complacent during a run of good luck – you never know when it will end. Good and bad luck nearly always balance themselves out in time. If there is an imbalance at the end of this life, it will be balanced out in the next life.

The apparent chaos of our life's events and the "random" fashion in which death, disease, and misfortune strikes, is an illusion. Scientists have now proved by new mathematics that "chaos" is actually governed by a beautiful pattern of order. The "Julia Set", a pictorial representation of chaos is stunning in its complexity and beauty. Scientists now believe that even the most unpredictable and chaotic events may be governed by simple laws (Laws of Karma?) and that these laws could be used to predict what was once unpredictable – such as our weather patterns. We are in a very exciting time where science and the paranormal are merging.

Stop crying "Why has this happened to me?" and "Why does God punish me like this?" and accept your karma. Ask instead, "Why have I been given this particular problem? What am I supposed to learn from it? What is it teaching me?" or, "Can I use my experience to help others in the same situation?" Remember, if God did answer your cries of "Why me?" He would say, "Because it is your karma and you must accept it and work it out." If you were then to say, "WHY is this my karma? It is not fair!" He would reply, "Why not?"

Life is a mixture of wormwood and honey and can never be all one or the other. And after the bitterness of the wormwood the honey tastes all the sweeter. No matter what you have been through there is always some good that can be gleaned from it. Almost all the charities that exist were founded by somebody whose personal tragedy or experience motivated them to set it up. Unless you have been shocked or moved by something you won't have the motivation to do something about it! The survivors of the Holocaust have the duty to educate the world about the evils of Anti-Semitism, prejudice, and fascism, and ensure that such a thing NEVER happens again.

Seek and seek until you find the reason for your particular problems. Many people who were sexually abused as children are now finding a voice and they are now in a postition to use their experiences to help others. Physical attack of any kind teaches you a lot about human strengths and weaknesses, and raises questions within you about aggression and sexuality. At the end of it all you are "older and wiser".

Try and look at everything from a positive rather than a negative view. This can be difficult, but you must persist. Soon the trials of life become challenges that you may actually welcome because of what you can learn from them. Each ordeal makes you that little bit more spiritually mature and each problem can be seen as grist to your mill.

However, once you have overcome your problems, and gleaned whatever you can from them, banish them forever into oblivion. They are over and gone and there is no need to let them interfere with your present life. There is a time to forgive and forget. A time to move on and accept changing circumstances.

When the Duke of Edinburgh went to Japan to attend Emperor Hirohito's funeral, many old war veterans were angry. They still bore a grudge against the Japanese for what happened to them in the insanity of war, even though it was forty-four years ago. A lot had changed in those forty-four years but they could not acknowledge those changes. And they had apparently forgotten the terrible suffering that was inflicted on the Japanese by the atom bombs. In war everyone suffers and war turns men into monsters. It is WAR that is the enemy! As far as Japan is concerned, we suffered, they suffered, and now we are square! It is time to forget the past, and use the lessons of war to make a better world for the future.

Animals live only for the present. They do not worry about the future, and (as far as we know) they don't brood over the past. Because of this they are much happier than we are and do not suffer all the stress-related illnesses that we have. Harry Emerson Fosdick said, "Hating people is like burning down your own house to get rid of a rat." In the end it is you who suffers, not the person you hate. If you are nursing any ancient grudges, this is the time to let them go.

This is the first day of a whole new life. A new dawn! Look forward from now on, not back. Put the pain of past events out of your mind and tell yourself it is all over now. All that matters is TODAY! NOW! Pretend you have amnesia, and what happened in the past is beyond recall. It was a bad dream, nothing more. Now you are waking from that dream and the sun is shining, and it is a brand new day. Do not allow the shadows of the past to rob you of happiness now. If disturbing thoughts of past events creep into your mind, tell them "Get out of my life! Go back where you came from! You're not going to hurt me anymore!"

Cultivate the fighting spirit by directing your anger at your depression and your own negativity, rather than at people or things in the world outside. See your depression as a malevolent black beast and exorcise it. Drive it right out of your life and fight it with everything you've got. This is where the Eight Point Plan comes in. The purpose of the plan is to make your body, your mind, and your home, utterly hostile to the black beast, so that it can no longer survive.

If you ever saw the film, "Gremlins" you will recall that the little creatures must not be fed after midnight, and must never get wet! Are you feeding your Black Beast after midnight? Are you taking it into the shower with you? Starve it! Dehydrate it! Flood it with brilliant white light! (Gremlins, remember, couldn't stand bright light.)

As soon as you hear the sadistic cackle of the gremlin inside you, delighting in your depression, take action. Have a good cry if you need to – science has proved that tears are good for you and you will feel a lot better afterwards. Then take an "antidote" to depression. Listen to some uplifting music, immerse yourself in a beloved hobby, get out in the garden, read something, take a long hot bath, and pamper yourself. Do whatever cheers you up.

A scrap book full of beautiful pictures cut from magazines and catalogues is a good fillip when you are feeling down. You don't have to be a child to keep a scrap book. Pictures of happy people, healthy people, animals, flowers, beautiful scenery, sunshine, tropical beaches, bowls of strawberries and cream – collect and keep pictures such as these in your scrap book. Collect positive affirmations too, and inspiring verses of poetry. These things are every bit as good as any pills the doctor gives you.

Sometimes it helps to retreat into happy memories, particularly those from your childhood. You could go through old photographs – but only the ones that make you smile. Activity such as jogging, swimming or dancing can help lift your spirits or a walk in the country or the nearest park. When out walking pay attention to what you see and don't brood on your problems. This is where a full knowledge of trees, wild flowers and birds comes in useful, because you might find something interesting. It can lift your spirits to discover a rare wild flower or an unusual tree in your locality. People in towns have the benefit of wonderful parks to explore. In a London park I was thrilled to discover a five hundred-year-old oak and a swamp cypress, and the flowerbeds in the park were filled with wonderfully scented Heliotropium or Cherry Pie. The flora and fauna of a city park can often be richer than that in the country, so don't knock parks!

Gastronomic treats can lift you out of a blue mood, but do not rely on food too often or you will get fat. A regular once a week treat does help however, and gives you something to look forward to for the rest of the week. Special ice cream, cream cakes, fresh strawberries or chocolate rum truffles make excellent "treat" foods and do no harm providing you stick to the Eight Point Plan wholefood diet the rest of the time. If you are weepy, why not make yourself a comforting drink? A cup of tea with some mint, or lemon balm, or bergamot in it; coffee with a capful of rum in it, hot chocolate with cinnamon, or real Irish coffee. Again, alcohol, if it is used in this way, should be strictly rationed. If you resort to alcohol for comfort too often you will soon have another problem as well as depression! Use your common sense. Alcohol has a place in strictly medicinal doses. It can remove inhibitions and enable a person to express grief or sorrow openly, and is useful therefore, if you find it difficult to cry. But I am talking about very occasional use. Abuse of alcohol will increase your depression and may push you over the edge into "Self-Destruct" so be very careful. If you have any doubt about your ability to control your alcohol intake then avoid it altogether!

Imagine yourself climbing the Ladder of Life one rung at a time. Keep climbing upwards and never allow yourself to slip down. Remember that however far down you feel you are on this ladder, if your keep climbing, even if your progress is painfully slow, eventually you must reach the top. Work on yourself constantly to change your attitude to life and chase away the apathy that chains you to the bottom of the ladder. Keep the top rung always in your sights, and keep climbing!

If you receive a blow and you slip down again, remember the One Day Rule. Allow yourself to lose one day wallowing in your misery and being negative, but keep in mind that tomorrow you are going to dry your eyes, pick yourself up, and resume your climb, even more determined than ever.

Start fresh every day, putting the negativity of the previous day behind you. Each dawn should be seen as a new beginning. Get up at dawn on bright summer days and watch the sun rise, listening to the birds singing with pure joy as a new day begins. Have you ever seen the sun rising? Have you ever been out in your garden at dawn? Dawn is the best time of day to walk in the garden and enjoy the peace and tranquillity that can be found, even in cities, at this time of day. It is also a good time to meditate. As you watch the rising sun tell yourself it is a new beginning for you, and you are putting the past behind you. You are at the dawn of a new life – a fuller and happier life. You'll damn well MAKE it a full and happy life and won't let depression stifle you any longer.

Constantly din it into yourself that you are driving the dark cloud away and purging yourself of negativity. When you wash yourself say "With these waters of life I wash away all negativity and all darkness", and see the sludge of negativity and depression going down the plug hole. Young girls used to wash their faces in morning dew on May-day, but you can wash your face in the dew any morning you choose. There is something magical about dew, for it condenses miraculously out of the air and vanishes as soon as the sun is up. It is an essence of the rising sun. Wash your face in the dew as you watch the sun rise, and wash away your negativity. Believe that it has the power to heal you of all sorrow and all illness.

Remember the power of light? Sunlight is the very stuff of life and you should get as much sunlight into your life as possible. Harness sunshine for healing purposes in any way you can – charge crystals in it, let it drive away the winter blues, and gather morning dew. Another way you can harness the power of the sun is to make a "Vita Florum" remedy. Take a Marigold flower (Calendula), and place it in a glass or crystal bowl filled with water. (Sundae dishes are best.) Try to use spring water for this but ordinary tap water will do if you cannot get spring water.

Choose a sunny day with the promise of several hours of unbroken sunshine ahead. Place the dish of water with the flower-head floating in it, in the sunniest place you can find, but somewhere it won't be upset. A low wall, sundial, or garden table are the most suitable places. Leave this in the sun for at least three hours, then go out to it and drink the water. You will find the water is filled with fizzy bubbles – the water has become charged with the prana in the sunlight and this has mingled with the essences from the flower. As you drink it you may feel a surge of energy going through you that is quite startling! Vita Florum remedies are similar to Bach Flower Remedies but they are easily made at home and cost nothing.

Marigolds are the best flower to use as they are ruled by the sun and moon and they inspire happiness and energy. Borage, honeysuckle, roses, and lavender can also be made into Vita Florum remedies. In each case the essence of the flower is combined with the sun-charged water to create a very powerful natural medicine. (Since Marigolds are edible you can eat the flower as well as drinking the water, if you so wish.)

Keep to the Eight Point Plan until it becomes second nature to you, gradually incorporating all its elements into your life, and throwing out old negative ways and negative habits. The effects of the plan are subtle, and only when ALL its elements become a way of life will you notice changes in your outlook on the world around you. Keep climbing the ladder – upwards, ever upwards. To slip back now is unthinkable. What is there down there but misery, despair, and death. Is that what you want?

Take up the challenge of life and make up your mind you are going to triumph over every adversity. Sometimes a situation becomes so intolerable that the only solution is drastic change – a move to a new house, a new area, a new job, or even a new country. Don't put up with intolerable conditions. Take the bull by the horns and change them! If crime is getting you down start a neighbourhood watch scheme. If housing conditions are the problem start a residents' association and fight. Do all you can to change the things that contribute to your depression, but if you cannot change them, consider moving away from them.

Work through your karma, accepting it with serenity and grace. Suffering should be seen as a sort of purgatory that cleanses the soul and enlightens you. Use your suffering to learn valuable lessons and to help others if possible. Depression and manic-depression are often the flip side of tremendous creativity, so find your creative talents and USE them.

Do not look down on yourself and despise yourself. You are no better and no worse than billions of other people. Low self-esteem is simply a manifestation of your illness, and is one of the negative attitudes you must fight. Make the most of yourself in every way you can and you will do okay.

A girlfriend of an acquaintance of mine was severely depressed and she was convinced she was stupid, even imagining she had suffered some kind of brain damage. Now, if you believe you are stupid, you will be. This is a fact that has been proved. "Hot House People" are proof that intelligence is flexible, and brain power can be increased if the brain is exercised, in the same way that muscles grow if you do weight-training. Depressed people simply have a lazy brain and responses are sluggish. The result is that you feel and act dull and unintelligent. But with active mental stimulation intelligence will increase and responses will sharpen. So "Hot House" yourself. Memorise the multiplication tables, Latin phrases, the Greek alphabet, the names of bones and muscles, the table of elements, verses of poetry, and anything else you can find that will exercise your brain. Read books that will teach you something new. Expand your brain-power and your horizons.

You will get nowhere by sitting and weeping in despair, or wallowing in negativity and being horrible to everybody. Take your life in your hands right now and make up your mind you are going to change. There is nothing to lose and everything to gain. Even if you feel like crawling away into a hole and dying, FORCE yourself, and give it everything you have got. You must have patience though. It could take a few years to make enough changes to see any improvement. The initial efforts are by far the hardest, but can you afford not to make them? Soon life will begin to regain its sparkle and you will realise you are more content, and even, dare you admit it, happy!

Fill your life with sunshine, bright colours, flowers, green plants, animals, beautiful music, good books, and poetry. All the positive things. And once a day carry out the meditation and visualisation exercises. The secret of happines lies within you, not out there in the outside world.

One day you will suddenly realise you are winning, and you are nearing the top of the ladder. You have dragged yourself up out of the quicksands of depression and at last you can see some light. The sun breaking through after a long night of darkness. Then you will say to yourself, "I've got a good life really, and everything is going to be all right!"

Appendix One

RELAXATION EXERCISES

FOR MAXIMUM EFFECT first massage the forehead, temples, back of neck, and stomach (just above the navel) with a relaxing aromatic oil. A good one you can make up is a mix of vetivert oil, chamomile oil, and lavender oil in a base of pure olive oil. If you cannot obtain all three essential oils then any one will suffice, diluted in olive oil and kept in a small bottle.

Finish the massage by pressing the heels of the hands sharply and firmly into the temples, then apply pressure to either side of the nasal bone with finger and thumb. This relaxes the muscles of the neck and scalp.

Begin relaxation by putting on some soothing music and lying down, making yourself completely comfortable. Eyes can be open and centred on the ceiling above, or closed, whatever you prefer. Begin breathing in very slowly and deeply, using the abdomen, not the chest. Imagine that air is being drawn in through your feet and is flowing up the legs in the form of a soft white mist. Once you can see and feel the air being drawn in through the feet, see it coming in through your hands in the same way.

Concentrate on the misty white luminescence filling your body and making you radiant with white light. On expiration, imagine the body cells have absorbed all the light and the air flowing outwards through nose, hands, and feet, is a dull greyish-brown with all the impurities it has washed out of your body. On inspiration you are inhaling both oxygen and prana, brilliant with life and healing; and on expiration you are exhaling carbon dioxide and all your pain, negativity, and illness.

While keeping up this visualisation, concentrate on each group of muscles in turn, starting at your feet and working upwards. Tell them to "Let go" and sink limply into the bed. Feel them growing heavier as you do so. When you have relaxed all your muscles, imagine yourself lying on a warm tropical beach, listening to the gentle swash of the waves on the shore. Hear the trickle of the water as the tide flows in and the crackle of shingle as it ebbs. Feel the hot sun on your body, the soft white sand beneath you, and the sea breezes ruffling your hair. Keep listening to the sound of your imaginary sea while you rest.

Sometimes, when we are very tense and nerves are on edge, all the relaxation exercises in the world fail to help. You may find you have trouble getting to sleep at night because your mind "races" and you toss and turn restlessly unable to settle. In situations like this a much stronger exercise is required.

Go into meditation as described in chapter nine, but when you are mentally relaxed, begin to rock with a fairly quick tempo (about once a second) from side to side or forwards and backwards, whatever you find most comfortable. It is much easier to do this in a crosslegged lotus posture – otherwise, sit upright in a chair. When you were a baby your mother rocked you whenever you were upset, and it invariably soothed you to sleep. Everyone knows rocking is soothing, but few people can say why. However, once you find the right rhythm it is extremely relaxing, and you may literally rock yourself to sleep.

If you are in a public situation or lying in bed where the rocking movement is difficult to perform, there is a more discreet version that is almost as effective. Hold something cool and hard in your hand, such as a pebble (the smoother the better) and squeeze it firmly then release. Keep doing this, in a sort of pumping motion, again at a speed of about once a second. (If you have ever given blood you will be familiar with this exercise, for they get you to do it to speed up the flow of blood.) You will find that a remarkable thing happens. As you begin squeezing your pebble, all the tension in the rest of your body simply melts away! Keep up a regular rhythm, and you will soon find your self drifting off into sleep without even trying. The more tense you are the harder you should squeeze the pebble. All the tension is then in the hand and the rest of your body is free from it.

Rocking can be used to deepen ordinary meditation and is a wonderfully relaxing and refreshing way of coping with stress. You will soon find there is a "natural" rhythm where little or no effort is required to maintain the motion and very little actual movement is required – no more than an inch or two each way. So rock away your tension and never let it get the better of you.

Appendix Two

"WAYS TO FILL EMPTY HOURS"

PEOPLE WHO ARE UNEMPLOYED, retired, sick or disabled, may find themselves with more time on their hands than they know what to do with. Filling empty hours in a way that is positive, constructive, and satisfying, is often a problem, and when apathy and depression set in there is a temptation to give up all activity and sit in an armchair all day or take to bed. If you are one of those people who complain, "But what can I DO?" here is a list of fifty-six activities suitable for just about anybody. Some of these have already been suggested, but there are many other activities listed here, most of which do not require a tremendous amount of physical energy.

1. Read a book on a subject that interests you.
2. Read a book about something completely new to you.
3. Try some drawing or painting.
4. Go beach-combing. Gather attractive pebbles for your garden parth or to put in a small basket indoors. If you don't know what types of rock make up the pebbles, get some books on rocks and minerals and find out. You will be amazed at the variety of different coloured pebbles there are. If pebbles do not excite you, search the beach for a "holed" stone which is considered lucky.
5. Look for a four-leaved clover in a field or park. They are not as rare as you might imagine.
6. Carve something from pieces of wood – lime or maple is best. Make little wooden amulets, jewellery, or ornaments.
7. Study the insect life in your garden. Entomology is a fascinating subject when you get into it. Can you name the butterflies and moths that visit your garden, and could you identify that strange beetle sunning itself on the path? Where do they go in winter, and what do they eat?

8. Listen to music – but REALLY LISTEN. Carry out relaxation exercises or meditate while you listen, or let the music conjure up pleasant scenes for you to immerse yourself in. Make up your own "albums" by taping collections of your records to suit different moods.

9. Gardening. Make your own garden a paradise on Earth, or get yourself an allotment.

10. Start studying and collecting crystals and minerals.

11. Make up a personal collection of your favourite poems, or write your own.

12. Write a story, whether or not you want to publish it.

13. Write an article for a magazine. If you have never written before but have "always wanted to", get a copy of the Writers & Artists Yearbook and read it through. Then start typing.

14. Sing something. Sing along to records, or get a song book and learn some songs. Join a choir if you find you enjoy singing.

15. Dance. Dance to records in your own home if you do not want to go to discos or classes.

16. Join a few charities and get involved in their activities.

17. Write lots of letters. Write to MPs about subjects on which you have strong feelings and write to magazine letter pages. Find some penpals to write to. Try and have at least one foreign penpal.

18. Bake or cook something special. Try sweet-making or bread-making, or discover Chinese or Indian cookery.

19. Try a new food – something you have never tasted before. Exotic tropical fruits, tofu (beancurd), tahini (sesame seed paste), carob (similar to chocolate but good for migraine sufferers as it doesn't cause migraine), coconut cream, chick peas, bamboo shoots – the list is endless. Search your local health food store.

20. Learn palmistry, or graphology, or study the Tarot cards or astrology.

21. Go out and do what you can for the stray dogs and cats. Cats – feed them, rescue any that are sick, hurt, or in kitten, and take them to the local PDSA or Cats Protection League clinic (which are free). Get them neutered or spayed and try to find homes for them. Dogs – feed them, then call the RSPCA. Our cities are full of unwanted pets who desperately need help. Do something for them.

22. Give help to a homeless person on the streets. Treat them to a good square meal and listen to their stories. See if you can help them find accommodation through such agencies as SHELTER and help them regain some self-respect. Even a meal or a cup of tea is better than nothing.

23. Examine your local Ordnance Survey map and explore anything interesting, such as a pond or river you have never seen, sites of special interest, ancient stone circles and ruined castles.
24. Try your hand at dowsing. You can get books from the library that will teach you how and you can make dowsing rods from wire coathangers.
25. Study astronomy and look at the stars. A pair of binoculars is every bit as good as a cheap telescope.
26. Hybridise flowers and fruit varieties in your garden. You could even start breeding roses if you are keen! You never know – you might breed a new rose that will make you famous.
27. Study pyramid power. Make or buy a pyramid and experiment with it.
28. Start a scapbook, using pictures cut out of magazines or old calendars.
29. Find out about other world religions and read their sacred texts.
30. Take up beekeeping. Get some books first, visit some beekeepers, then join a beekeeper's association in your area. They will advise you. Beekeeping is an ideal hobby for the newly retired, and can become totally absorbing. There is the added bonus of honey. Many colleges run beekeeping courses for beginners – enquire.
31. Start train or plane spotting. Go to your local airport and watch the planes taking off and landing. If you can afford it why not take some flying lessons?
32. Get a CB radio and tune in to all the other CB users in your area.
33. Experiment with psychic healing and "mind over matter" healing techniques. Some suitable books will help.
34. Try sending telepathic messages to a friend.
35. Clear out your attic or cellar. You never know what might be hidden under the cobwebs.
36. Go to jumble sales or auctions and see what you can find.
37. If you have a mechanical bent, take in clocks, bicycles, or cars, and repair them.
38. Learn yoga and practise it every day. It can do you a lot of good.
39. Learn "T'ai-chi" or Chinese massage techniques. A good book to start you off on Taoist healing methods is "Burn Disease out of Your Body" by Stephen T. Chang with Richard C. Miller. There is enough in here to keep you occupied for hours every day.
40. Collect "Folklore".
41. Explore your "Inner Planes". Carry out imaginary journeys in your mind. This is a form of meditation.

42. Read the Mahabharata and the Ramayana.
43. Learn a language using either tapes or books.
44. Study numerology. What is your lucky number and what is your unlucky number? What is the number of your name?
45. Start a collection of something. Stamps, beermats, or something more unusual.
46. Sew or knit. Get a knitting machine and design and sell your own knitwear.
47. Raise trees, shrubs, and herbaceous periennials from seed and give the surplus away or hold plant sales to raise money for charity.
48. Make your own beer or wine. Start with kits, then try doing it with raw ingredients.
49. Get into aromatherapy. Make up massage/healing oils from essential oils in a base of olive oil.
50. Search for fossils.
51. Go birdwatching, or just watch the birds in your garden, after building a five star bird breeding station opposite a window.
52. Women – pamper yourself. Give yourself a complete facial (a good face pack can be made from Fuller's Earth, oatmeal, honey and milk) then give your hair a hot oil treatment using warm olive or coconut oil. Follow this up with "body-brushing" and a luxurious bath or shower. You will feel (and look) wonderful after this.
53. Men – Get yourself in shape. Do some body building to give yourself muscles, either at a health club or at home. If your hair is turning grey and you don't like it, dye it. There are now hair dyes for men as well as women. You will be amazed at how a little hair dye can take years off you. Grow a beard if you think it will make you look better, or, if you already have one, shave it off! Try whatever you can to make yourself look good.
54. Learn to swim and go swimming regularly.
55. Learn calligraphy (fancy handwriting) and offer to do posters etc. for local functions.
56. Make a weather station in your garden and start recording the weather. Weather is always interesting and a mini weather station is not an expensive thing to build. It could even be placed on a balcony if you live in a high rise flat, or on the roof. Start keeping a weather diary.